W9-CNQ-323

edition

Using IBM® SPSS® Statistics
for Social Statistics *and*
Research Methods

For my sister, Becky, and my brother, Ben

3rd edition

Using IBM® SPSS® Statistics for Social Statistics and Research Methods

William E. Wagner, III
California State University, Channel Islands

Los Angeles | London | New Delhi
Singapore | Washington DC

For information:

Pine Forge Press
An Imprint of SAGE
   Publications, Inc.
2455 Teller Road
Thousand Oaks, California 91320
E-mail: order@sagepub.com

SAGE Publications India Pvt. Ltd.
B 1/I 1 Mohan Cooperative
   Industrial Area
Mathura Road, New Delhi 110 044
India

SAGE Publications Ltd.
1 Oliver's Yard
55 City Road
London, EC1Y 1SP
United Kingdom

SAGE Publications
   Asia-Pacific Pte. Ltd.
33 Pekin Street #02–01
Far East Square
Singapore 048763

Printed in the United States of America

Library of Congress Cataloging-in-Publication Data

Wagner, William E. (William Edward)
Using IBM® SPSS® Statistics for social statistics and research methods / William E. Wagner, III. — 3rd ed.
    p. cm.
ISBN 978-1-4129-9142-1 (pbk. : acid-free paper) 1. Social sciences—Statistical methods. 2. SPSS for Windows. I. Title.
HA32.W34 2011
300.285′555—dc22   2010032253
This book is printed on acid-free paper.

10   11   12   13   14   10   9   8   7   6   5   4   3   2   1

Acquisitions Editor:	Jerry Westby
Editorial Assistant:	Nichole O'Grady
Production Editor:	Libby Larson
Copy Editor:	Cate Huisman
Typesetter:	C&M Digitals (P) Ltd
Proofreader:	Jenifer Kooiman
Cover Designer:	Glenn Vogel
Marketing Manager:	Erica DeLuca
Permissions Editor:	Karen Ehrmann

Contents

Preface

This book was written for those learning introductory statistics or with some basic statistics knowledge who want to use SPSS/PASW Statistics software to manage data and/or carry out basic statistical analyses. It can also be a useful tool to gain an understanding of how SPSS/PASW Statistics software works before going on to more complicated statistical procedures. This volume is an ideal supplement for a statistics or research methods course. While it can be used with any research methods or statistics book or materials, it was tailored to complement *Investigating the Social World,* by Russell Schutt (2009), and *Social Statistics for a Diverse Society,* by Chava-Frankfort Nachmias and Anna Leon-Guerrero (2009). It can also be used as a guide for those working with basic statistics on their own. The book provides information for users about some of the important mechanics of SPSS/PASW Statistics operating procedures for simple data management along with accessible introductory instructions to statistical operations.

References

Frankfort-Nachmias, C., & Leon-Guerrero, A. (2009). *Social statistics for a diverse society* (5th ed.). Thousand Oaks, CA: Pine Forge Press.

Schutt, R. (2009). *Investigating the social world* (6th ed.). Thousand Oaks, CA: Pine Forge Press.

Acknowledgments

Many thanks go to Jerry Westby at SAGE/Pine Forge Press for his support and vision. Anna Leon-Guerrero and Russell Schutt were particularly helpful, providing insightful reviews and productive suggestions for the second edition.

The author and SAGE gratefully acknowledge the contributions of the following reviewers:

Safiya Omari, Jackson State University

Yanyan Sheng, Southern Illinois University Carbondale

Robert Silverman, University at Buffalo

1

Overview

This book serves as a guide for those interested in using IBM SPSS/PASW Statistics software to aid in statistical data analysis— whether as a companion to a statistics or research methods course or as a stand-alone guide for a particular project or individual learning. The images and directions used in this book come from SPSS/PASW Statistics Version 18.0, first released in the autumn of 2009.

What's the Difference Between SPSS Statistics and PASW Statistics? None

There is essentially no difference. The program formerly known simply as "SPSS" became "SPSS Statistics" with the Version 17.0 release, and then "PASW Statistics" with the Version 18.0 release. After SPSS, Inc. became an IBM company in October of 2009, the branding going forward was changed, so that future releases of the software (Version 19.0 and beyond) will be known as "IBM SPSS Statistics." When SPSS was originally developed, it stood for Statistical Package in the Social Sciences. The motivation for the PASW (Predictive Analytics Software) branding change was to reflect the considerable reach of the software to more business-oriented realms, although this name is used only for Version 18.

Statistical Software

The SPSS/PASW Statistics software works with several kinds of computer files: data files, output files, and syntax files. *Data files* are those computer files that contain the information that the user intends to analyze. *Output files* contain the statistical analysis of these data, often displayed as tables, graphs, and/or charts. *Syntax files* are computer instructions that tell the SPSS/PASW Statistics software what to do. Syntax files are not used with the student version of SPSS/PASW Statistics and are dealt with as an advanced application in Chapter 12 of this book.

The General Social Survey (GSS) serves the secondary dataset used to demonstrate typical functions of the program by example. SPSS/PASW Statistics is the software program, produced by SPSS, an IBM company as of 2009, in Chicago, Illinois. The GSS is a dataset that is read and analyzed by the SPSS/PASW Statistics software; it is a data file containing the information to be analyzed. The two things are distinct and can be used in separate contexts without the other.

About the General Social Survey (GSS) Data

The National Opinion Research Center (NORC) at the University of Chicago administers the GSS. The GSS was started in 1972 and continues to the present time. The data used for the examples in this book come from the latest available completed version of the GSS collected in 2008. According to NORC, with the exception of the U.S. Census, the GSS is the most frequently analyzed source of information in the social sciences. NORC acknowledges that there are at least 14,000 instances where the GSS has been used for articles in scholarly journals, books, and doctoral dissertations. Further, it is estimated that over 400,000 students annually use the GSS in their work.

The GSS contains many demographic and attitudinal questions, as well as rotating topics of special interest. A number of core questions have remained unchanged in each survey since 1972. This allows for rich longitudinal research about the attitudes, opinions, and demographics in the United States. Topical questions appear sometimes for just one year; other times, they can appear for a period of years. Therefore, the GSS is versatile as a longitudinal data resource and a relevant cross-sectional resource.

To maximize the amount of information that can be collected in this massive interviewing project, the GSS uses a *split ballot design,* in which NORC asked some questions in only a random subsample of the households and asked other questions in other households. Some questions, including demographic items, were asked of all respondents. When we begin analyzing the GSS data, you will notice that some data items have a substantial number of respondents for whom data are marked as missing. For the most part, this refers to respondents who were not asked that particular question as a result of the split ballot design.

Although many items were asked of only a subsample of respondents, you can still take the responses as representative of the U.S. adult noninstitutionalized population, subject to normal sampling error. For more information about how the GSS data were collected, see Appendix B, Field Work and Interviewer Specifications, and Appendix C, General Coding Instructions, in the *General Social Survey 1972–2008 Cumulative Codebook* (Davis, Smith, & Marsden, 2009).

SPSS/PASW Electronic Files

PASW Statistics 18 (as well as other versions of SPSS Statistics) uses different file extensions, or *endings*, and associated icons to signify types of files. For instance, a file named "file.sav" is a data file called "file." The ".sav" is used to signify that this is a data file. Again, data files contain the information that SPSS/PASW Statistics is used to analyze. A file with the extension ".sps," is an SPSS/PASW Statistics syntax file, while a file with the extension ".spv" (or ".spo" for older versions of SPSS software prior to Version 17.0) is an SPSS/PASW Statistics output file. Output files contain analyses of data, such things as charts, tables, and other statistical and data manipulation information. Syntax files contain coded instructions for SPSS/PASW Statistics to perform operations on data and to produce output. It is not necessary to create, save, or even deal with syntax files for most basic SPSS/PASW Statistics functions; therefore, syntax files will be covered only to the level of description and simple use in Chapter 12.

Opening Existing Data Files

To open an SPSS/PASW Statistics data file that you already have or have obtained, select the "File" menu, then choose "Open," and select "Data." (For other file types, see the section on importing data from non–SPSS/PASW file formats.) At this point you will need to navigate the disk drives (or network drives or other sorts of storage devices) to locate the data file that you wish to open. Once you locate the file, either double click on it, or click on it once and then click the "Open" button toward the bottom right side of the "Open File" dialog box.

SPSS/PASW Statistics will then open the data file, and you will be presented with the information in a grid format (somewhat similar to a Microsoft Excel or other spreadsheet environment). You have choices about both the way the information is presented and the information you see. For example, you can choose to see the Data View, presented in the following image. Here, you are viewing the actual data. Note that the variables are listed in columns with each case recorded as a row. The variable "age" has been selected as a reference point. The data in that column tell the ages of each of the respondents.

Now, click on the Variable View tab, which is located toward the bottom left of the screen. (Note that the Data View tab is currently selected; this is the default when opening a new file with SPSS or PASW Statistics 17 or 18.) While the information looks somewhat different, you are still looking at the same data file. See the following image:

Again, the "age" variable has been selected for reference. In this view, variables are depicted in rows, with each row showing information about a single variable, such as variable label, category label, type, level of measurement, and so forth. You can add to, edit, or delete any of the variable information contained in this view by directly typing into the cells. This view does not show the actual response data; to view that you would need to select the Data View option.

Importing Data From Non–SPSS/PASW Statistics File Formats

There is often a need to analyze existing data files that were not created or formatted by SPSS/PASW Statistics software. These files might be created by other statistical software packages (e.g., SAS or Stata,) or by other types of numeric operational programs (e.g., Microsoft Excel). To open these files, first select the same menu options you would if you were opening an SPSS/PASW Statistics data file:

FILE → OPEN → DATA

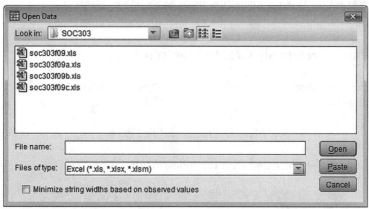

Now, at the "Files of type" prompt at the bottom of the dialog box, click the arrow at the right to expand the choices. Next, select "Excel (*.xls, *.xlsx, *.xlsm)." You will need to navigate your hard drive, other drives, or other locations to find your file. Once you locate the file, select and open it. At this point, you will be presented with a new dialog box:

If the column headings in the Microsoft Excel file contain the variable names, then make sure the box asking to "Read variable names from the first row of data" is selected. If the column headings are not formatted in a way that conforms to the SPSS/PASW Statistics variable-naming conventions, then they will be transformed into permitted variable names, and the original names will be recorded as variable labels.

To import only a portion of the Excel file, then enter the range of cells from which you would like to import data.

It is also possible to import files from databases, text files, and other sources. Follow the same instructions as with Excel files, except for the file type you select. Depending on the file type you choose, you will be presented with different dialog boxes or wizards to import the data and process it for use by SPSS/PASW Statistics.

In some cases, you may simply have unlabeled data in a particular file, or the variable names or other information may be of little or no use to you. In that case, depending upon the size of the file, you could copy the data from the original numeric program (e.g., Microsoft Excel), and then paste it directly into the SPSS/PASW Statistics Data View window. This is particularly useful if you just want to add numeric values from another source and enter or program the other information using SPSS/PASW Statistics.

Opening Previously Created Output Files

In order to open a previously created output file, select from the "File" menu as follows:

FILE → OPEN → OUTPUT

You will be presented with the following dialog box:

Here, just navigate to find your file, as you would any other type of file. Once you locate it, select and open the file. SPSS/PASW Statistics will open the file into an Output Viewer window. There, you can view and edit it. Note that Version 18 (as well as Versions 16 and 17) of SPSS/PASW Statistics uses the *.spv file extension. Earlier versions of SPSS software employ the *.spo file extension. SPSS/PASW Version 18 is capable of opening output files created with older versions of SPSS software, but files created in the new version can not necessarily be opened in the older versions.

Saving Files

All types of SPSS/PASW Statistics files are saved in virtually the same way as files in any modern computer program. Select either

FILE → SAVE   to save the file as the currently assigned name,

or

FILE → SAVE AS   to save the file in a different file,
under a new name.

The first option above will automatically save the file without prompting you for a dialog box, unless you are working with a new, yet unnamed, file. In that case, you will get the same type of dialog box as though you had selected the "Save As" option. If you do choose the second option, you will be given a dialog box prompting you to name the file and to select the location on your computer or network where the file is to be placed.

Creating New SPSS/PASW Statistics Data Files

To create a new SPSS/PASW Statistics data file, select the "File" menu; then choose "New," and select "Data":

FILE → NEW → DATA

You will then be presented with a blank Data Editor window like the one following.

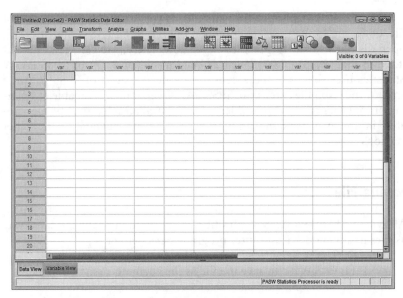

You can immediately start entering information related to the variables you wish to create and/or the actual data codes that you may have. In the Data Editor window that follows, the Variable View tab has been selected and information has been entered for two variables: AGE and SEX. Notice that the labels have been entered: "Respondent's age" and "Respondent's sex," respectively. Other information about the variables has been selected and entered, as well.

For the SEX variable, value labels have been entered. This was done by clicking on the "Values" cell for that variable and then selecting the button with three small dots. The following dialog box would have appeared.

In the "Value Labels" box, you can enter the label for each of the category codes for the variable. In this case, "0" was entered in the "Value" box, while "female" was entered into the "Label" box. At that point, to record the information, it is necessary to click the "Add" button. Notice, also, that "1" was entered into the "Value" box and "male" was entered into the "Label" box, and again, the "Add" button was clicked. (This procedure also produces a dummy variable called "male," where the value of 1 is male, and 0 is "not male.") By doing this, we are assigning numbers to the categories of the variable, SEX, so that SPSS/PASW Statistics knows how to record whether the respondent is male or female; the software uses numbers to keep track of those attributes. By using numbers, the software can track the categories and use that information to perform statistical operations such as those described throughout this book.

It is also possible to enter the data directly into the Data Editor. To do this, click the Data View tab at the lower left of the Data Editor window. The columns now represent the newly created variables: AGE and SEX. You can directly type the values for each case or row. You could also copy (<Ctrl> + C in Windows, or <Apple> + C on a Macintosh) and paste (<Ctrl> + V in Windows, or <Apple> + V on a Macintosh) these values from another software program, such as Microsoft Excel, if you already have them typed categorized by the same variables.

Notice that the data entered (or pasted) above appear as the numeric codes that were assigned for nominal and ordinal variables that have those assignments. There is a way to have the actual label shown in this window. Click the following from the SPSS/PASW menus, and note the differences in the screen image below:

VIEW → VALUE LABELS

Value labels can also be displayed prior to entering data. When you double click on the right side of a cell, an arrow will appear. If you click on the arrow, as seen in the screen image above, a pull down menu consisting of all of the available categories for that variable will appear: In this case, the list consists of "female" and "male." If you are entering data directly into SPSS/PASW Statistics, using this option can make data entry easier and can help avoid error, such as typos of values that are not within the range of categories for a variable.

Creating and Editing
SPSS/PASW Statistics Output Files

Output files are created by SPSS/PASW Statistics when you instruct the software to perform functions. For example, if you request SPSS/PASW Statistics to provide frequencies and central tendency values for three variables from your dataset, then an output file will automatically be produced. The information that you have requested will be presented in the Output Viewer window, unless an output file is already open in the Output Viewer, in which case the new information will be appended to that file. To edit the output, you'll select and double click the part you wish to work with, and there are tools to facilitate that task. More information on this topic will be provided in Chapter 4: Organization and Presentation of Information.

Preferences: Getting Started

To change the settings, parameters, and preferences for the SPSS/PASW Statistics program, select the "Edit" menu and choose "Options":

EDIT → OPTIONS

You will be given a dialog box like the one shown here:

There are numerous features that can be controlled using this dialog box, and most are intuitive in their operation. As a user becomes more experienced, he or she often utilizes more of these features. From the start, however, most SPSS/PASW Statistics users will want to make sure that variables will be displayed throughout the program in alphabetical order and also by name (rather than label). This can be done by selecting the "General" tab, and clicking the radio buttons for "Display names" and "Alphabetical."

This is particularly important if you are using or creating a dataset that contains a large number of variables, such as the General Social Survey. While it is clear that alphabetizing the list will facilitate easier access to variables, listing by name is also crucial, since variable labels are more detailed and may not necessarily begin with or even use the same letters as the variable name. Changing or verifying these settings up front can save a good deal of time and frustration. If a dataset is opened and the preferences have not been set to the desired parameters, the user can still go to the dialog box and make the change while the dataset is open. (In some older versions of SPSS, it would be necessary to close the dataset, make the change, and reopen the dataset.)

If you have started a procedure and don't wish to change the program preferences as described above, you can do it on the fly. Just right click (or <Option> + Click for Macintosh computers with a standard one-button mouse) one or more of the variables from the list shown in the dialog box with which you are working. You can select "Display Variable Names" and the "Sort Alphabetically." Incidentally, you can also select "Variable Information" for any of the variables (not more than one at a time), which will provide details about values, value labels, and so forth.

Note that this procedure, pictured above, will make the change only in the current dialog box (including return visits to that same dialog box, "Frequencies" in this case). You will need to use the same procedure to organize variables in other dialog boxes, or make the change at the program preferences window (EDIT → OPTIONS . . .). Also, note that this procedure does not work in all windows (e.g., UTILITIES → VARIABLES, see next paragraph).

To get a quick overview of the variables in a given dataset, SPSS/PASW Statistics has a variable utility window to provide useful information about each of the variables in a way that can be easily navigated (and such that information can be easily pasted to output if desired). Opening this window will demonstrate the importance of organized naming and ordering of variables in a large data file. Choose the "Utilities" menu; then select "Variables":

UTILITIES → VARIABLES

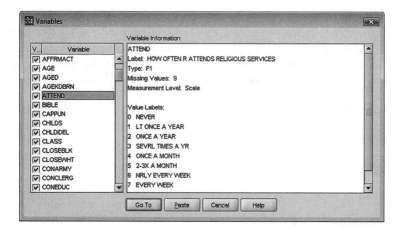

When you select a variable from the alphabetized list of variable names on the left, information about that particular variable will appear on the right side of the box, including the label, the level of measurement, and the value labels. This is a fast way to determine what kind of variables are available in your dataset that are suited to different statistical methods of analysis.

Measurement of Variables Using SPSS/PASW Statistics

Whether creating a new data file with SPSS/PASW Statistics or using an existing data file, it is important to understand how variables have been measured, or "treated," by the creator of the data file. This "treatment" is a factor of how the data were collected—how much information is contained within the dataset about each variable.

First, it is important to be aware that SPSS/PASW Statistics can record variables as either *string* variables or *numeric* variables. String variables can consist of letters and/or numbers and cannot be treated numerically; therefore, string variables must be treated at the nominal level of measurement. Numeric variables use numbers to represent response values. These numbers may represent actual numbers, ranked categories, or unranked categories. In other words, numeric variables may be *nominal, ordinal, interval,* or *ratio*.

In social science statistics and research methods courses, variables are typically described using these four categories. Many textbooks, such as *Investigating the Social World* (Schutt, 2009) or *Adventures in Social Research* (Babbie, Halley, Wagner, & Zaino, 2010) elaborate all four of those categories. In some texts, interval and ratio measures are combined, as is the case in *Social Statistics for a Diverse Society* (Frankfort-Nachmias & Leon-Guerrero, 2009).

SPSS/PASW Statistics uses the following codes for levels of measurement: nominal, ordinal, and scale. You can select the level of measurement from the pull down menu for each variable in the "Measure" column of the Variable View window. "Nominal" and "Ordinal" both correspond to the concepts with the same names. The "Scale" denotation corresponds to interval-ratio, interval, and ratio. There are functions within the SPSS/PASW Statistics software that will limit your ability to conduct analyses or create graphs based on the recognized level of measurement. Therefore, it is important to verify that the indicator in the "Measure" column of the Variable View is correct for all variables you will use in your analyses.

References

Babbie, E., Halley, F., Wagner, W. E., III, & Zaino, J. (2010). *Adventures in social research: Data analysis using IBM® SPSS® Statistics* (7th ed.). Thousand Oaks, CA: Pine Forge Press.

Davis, J. A., Smith, T. W., & Marsden, P. V. (2009). *General Social Surveys, 1972–2008: Cumulative codebook.* Chicago: National Opinion Research Center.

Frankfort-Nachmias, C., & Leon-Guerrero, A. (2009). *Social statistics for a diverse society* (5th ed.). Thousand Oaks, CA: Pine Forge Press.

Schutt, R. (2009). *Investigating the social world* (6th ed.). Thousand Oaks, CA: Pine Forge Press.

2

Transforming Variables

In this chapter, tools for restructuring variables will be introduced. SPSS/PASW Statistics allows for numerous ways to reconfigure, combine, and compute variables in a dataset.

Recoding and Computing Variables

Often, one must reorganize the way data are recorded before performing statistical analyses. This might be due to the level of measurement of a particular variable that a researcher wishes to change, or it could be related to the researcher's intended use of a variable. One may wish to collapse a few categories of a variable into one for appropriateness of analysis. For example, within the marital status variable, one might combine "married" and "separated" categories to form "legally married," and combine "divorced" with "single never married" to form "unmarried." "Recode" is the SPSS/PASW Statistics function that allows the researcher to recategorize the variable to suit the needs of the analysis.

There are many times when a researcher needs to produce a new variable from existing information in a dataset, but that information is not contained solely within one variable. SPSS/PASW Statistics has a "Compute" function that allows a user to both perform mathematical operations on variable data and to combine data from multiple distinct variables within the file.

For this recoding example, we will use the General Social Survey (GSS) 2008 dataset. We will take a straightforward case of dichotomizing age from a ratio variable, presenting the respondent's actual age at the time of interview, into just two categories with a cut point of 50 years of age. This would allow the researcher to present ages in a small frequency table, whereas before recoding age, there are so many categories (18 to 89 years of age) that presentation in a frequency table is not feasible. In order to recode, or change the categories of a variable, select the "Transform" menu, then choose the "Recode" option, and then select "Into Different Variables":

TRANSFORM → RECODE INTO DIFFERENT VARIABLES . . .

You will then be given a dialog box like the one displayed here:

It is useful and proactive against data loss to recode into "different variables," rather than "same variables" if you are reducing information contained within the variable. For instance, if you are recoding a ratio level variable into an ordinal or a dichotomous variable, then you would want to create a different variable. The reason behind this is that the lost information resulting from the recode would still be retained in the original variable should you want to change the way in which you recode the variable at some point later in time, or should you determine that you need the more detailed ratio level information for your analysis.

Recoding Variables: Dichotomies and Dummy Variables

In this example we recode the age variable into a dichotomy: a variable with exactly two categories, not including missing values. A dummy variable is a dichotomy usually coded with a value of "1" to indicate the existence of a particular attribute. All other attributes are coded to "0" as an indication that the particular attribute from "1," and usually the name of the variable itself, is not present. Dummy variables are particularly useful for including nominal level variables in analyses requiring interval or ratio level variables to perform statistical operations, including multiple regression models (see

Chapter 7: Correlation and Regression Analysis). It is also possible to use a series of dummy variables to represent several attributes from a given nominal variable.

To dichotomize the age variable, first select "age" from the list of variables in the dataset on the left, and then click the arrow to drag it to the "Numeric Variable" pane. Now, create a new name for the variable; in this example, the mundane "age2" has been conjured. You may also select a label at this time, or you can attend to that at a later time through the Variable View tab of the Data Editor screen. For this example, the label "age 50 & over, or not" was added. While it has not been done yet in the screen image above, the next step is to click the "Change" key. This will enter the name "age2" into the "Output Variable" location, where there is currently a "?" acting as a placeholder.

Now, it is necessary to give SPSS/PASW Statistics the instructions for *how* the variable is to be recoded. In this example, we want to change all ages up to and including 49 into a category, call it "0," and all ages 50 and greater into another category, call it "1." Click on the "Old and New Values" key in the "Recode into Different Variables" dialog box, and another dialog box will appear on top, like the one that follows:

To implement the changes, first, under "Old Value," select the radio button that reads, "Range, LOWEST through value." Then enter "49" in the box underneath. Then under "New Value" select "Value" and enter "0." Now, click the "Add" button. This instructs SPSS/PASW Statistics to transform all ages up to and including 49 into the category "0."

Next, under "Old Value" select the radio button associated with "Range, value through HIGHEST." Enter "50" in the box beneath that heading. Then, under "New Value," select "Value" and enter "1." Again, click the "Add" button. This now instructs SPSS/PASW Statistics to transform all ages 50 and beyond into the category "1."

Also, under "Old Value," select "System- or user-missing." Under "New Value" select "System-missing." This will ensure that missing values continue to be treated as such, even if they had been recorded as numeric values. Click the "Add" button once again to confirm that this instruction is added to the list.

Now your instructions have been entered, and you can click the "Continue" button; this will close the current dialog box and return you to the original "Recode into Different Variables" dialog box. Once there, you must click the "OK" button for SPSS/PASW Statistics to process your request to recode and then create the new variable.

If the "OK" is dimmed and SPSS/PASW Statistics will not allow you to click on it, then one of the above steps must not have been completed. The one most often overlooked is the requirement to click on the "Change" button, which adds the new variable name for the output variable.

After you have completed the recode, notice that the new variable is appended to the bottom of the variable list in the Variable View of the Data Editor window. It also happens that the variable is appended to the end (all the way to the right) of the Data View. You can move that variable to another place in the list if you wish by first selecting its entire row and then dragging the row (represented by a red line) up the screen to place it between two of the other variables above. In fact, you can change the "file order" of any of the variables if you wish. This might have utility for you if, for instance, you would like two or more variables to be near each other to compare or verify values in the Data View window.

For the variable information, you may wish to change the width from 8 (the default) to 1, since all possible values are only one digit, including missing case options, such as "IAP" or "Inapplicable" (7), "DK" or "Don't know" (8), and "NA" or "No answer" (9). Similarly, there are no decimals for this variable, so change the decimal column from 2 to 0. Since this variable is dichotomous, select "Nominal" under the "Measure" column.

Now, since this is a newly created variable, it is very important to insert value labels. If the variable label and/or value labels are not clear, then it can be easy to forget what the values are, or in which direction the variable was coded, thereby making the data unusable. Click the cell in the "Values" column for the variable to which you want to append value labels. Then click the button with three dots. The "Value Labels" dialog box will appear:

As before with value labels, enter both the value and the label. Then click the "Add" button after each value and label that you enter. When all value/label combinations have been entered, then click "OK." The value labels will then be updated. You can inspect the value labels in the Variable View window by clicking on the button with three dots on it in the "Values" column of the variable "age2."

Recoding Using Two or More Variables to Create a New Variable

Suppose you want to create a new variable of race/ethnicity that includes information from the variable "race," as well as the variable "Hispanic." The variable "race" includes only three categories: "White," "Black," and "Other." We want to select out those who identify as "Hispanic" and create a fourth category labeled as such.

In this example, we are going to "recode" the race variable into itself, using information from the variable "Hispanic." If you would like to preserve the original variable, "race," you can do that by duplicating it first; you might call it "race3," since there are three categories.

Let's begin. Select the following menus in SPSS/PASW Statistics:

TRANSFORM → RECODE INTO SAME VARIABLES . . .

Once the "Recode into Same Variables" dialog box appears, select and move the "race" variable to the "Numeric Variables" slot.

Now, click on "Old and New Values." Here, you will make the following entry: Old values from "1" through "3" will be routed to the new value of "4." See the following image to verify your entry. Then click "Continue."

If you think about the logic of what we have just done, we have recoded all respondents (regardless of whether they selected "1," "2," or "3" on the "race" variable) to "Hispanic." But we actually want to recode only the respondents who reported that they were Hispanic. So, let's add that condition to our SPSS/PASW Statistics command now. Click the "If" button in the "Recode into Same Variables" dialog box, and you will be presented with the following dialog box:

First, select the radio button associated with "Include if case satisfies condition." Now, find the variable "Hispanic" in the list on the left, and click the right-pointing arrow to send it to the slot under "Include if case satisfies condition." Since the variable "Hispanic" is coded "1" for not Hispanic and the values "2"–"50" indicate different types of Hispanic recognition, we want to include those cases where the respondent selected the number "2" or higher. So, click ">=" then "2." The equation is complete, and you should click "Continue" and then "OK" in the prior dialog box.

Since we have added a new category, it will be necessary to add the additional value label, as illustrated in the following dialog box. Remember that we get this box by going to the Variable View tab of the Data Editor window, finding the cell in the "Value Labels" column for the variable "race," and clicking the button with the three dots.

Click "OK" to add the new value label. Now, in order to verify that the recode was done correctly, request a frequency distribution of the new race variable:

ANALYZE → DESCRIPTIVE STATISTICS → FREQUENCIES . . .

race RACE OF RESPONDENT

		Frequency	Percent	Valid Percent	Cumulative Percent
Valid	1 WHITE	1429	70.6	70.6	70.6
	2 BLACK	272	13.4	13.4	84.1
	3 OTHER	85	4.2	4.2	88.3
	4 HISPANIC	237	11.7	11.7	100.0
	Total	2023	100.0	100.0	

You can also ask for frequency distributions of the original race variable, "race3," along with the variable "Hispanic," to verify that the recode was done properly. The distribution above reveals that the recode was carried out as we intended.

Computing Variables

There are numerous reasons why a user of SPSS/PASW Statistics would be interested in computing a new variable. For example, one may want to construct an index from individual questions, or one may wish to compute the logarithmic (log) function of a particular variable. In this example, we want to compute the average education level of the respondents' parents.

So, we will add the value for mother's education level to that for father's education level and then divide by two. (In more sophisticated approaches, we might divide by the number of parental responses.)

To perform the computation, select these menus:

TRANSFORM → COMPUTE...

The "Compute Variable" dialog box will be presented:

Type the name you wish to assign to the new variable in the "Target Variable" box; in this example "parentED" was chosen. Next, prepare the computation equation in the "Numeric Expression" box. In this case it is necessary to select the parentheses button, ( ), first. Then insert the "maeduc" variable by clicking the arrow to the right of the list of variables. Then insert an addition sign by clicking on the appropriate button beneath the "Numeric Expression" box. Now, add the "paeduc" variable into the parentheses, as well. Next, insert a divisor bar after the parentheses by clicking the button for such, and then click the number "2." This has the effect of adding together the total years of education of both parents and then dividing by two, yielding the average.

For users who are more comfortable with this process, note that you can type the expression directly into the "Numeric Expression" box that you wish SPSS/PASW Statistics to calculate. In this case, you could have typed the expression "(maeduc + paeduc) / 2" using your computer keyboard. If you use this method, be very careful to get the spelling of the variable names exactly correct, or SPSS/PASW Statistics will not be able to execute your command.

The "Type & Label" button opens a small dialog box that offers an immediate opportunity to enter a variable label and also to define the type of variable (e.g., numeric).

Note the functions that are available: Each selection in the "Function group" pane will bring up a separate list of functions in the "Functions and Special Variables" pane in the lower right corner of the "Compute Variable" box. There are statistical, trigonometric, date, time, string, and other functions that can be used to compute just about anything. Also, if you wish to set up a conditional computation—such that a computation is made in only one case, or there are to be different computations for different cases based on some predetermined condition, then select the "If" button in the lower left corner, and enter that/those condition(s). The same functions and keypads are provided to instruct SPSS/PASW Statistics how to determine the criteria for the conditional computation.

Using the Count Function

SPSS/PASW Statistics allows users the option to add up particular values across different variables. Suppose a researcher wanted to count up the number of instances where a respondent gave a "yes" answer to particular questions. For this example, consider the GSS (2008) series of questions on opinions relating to abortion. Use the menus below to carry out this example:

TRANSFORM → COUNT VALUES WITHIN CASES . . .

In the dialog box that appears, move the appropriate variables from the variable list on the left into the "Numeric Variables" box. It will also be necessary to enter a name for the new variable to be created in the "Target Variable" slot. The target label can be conveniently entered in the appropriate slot, as well. Next, click the "Define Values" button. The following dialog box will be provided:

Here, you will want to select the values to be counted. For the opinion questions that have been selected in this example, a code of "1" indicates an affirmative response (while a "2" indicates a negative response). Therefore, you want to count the number of responses that have a value of "1." Click the radio button next to "Value" at the upper left of the dialog box, and then enter a "1" into the associated slot beneath. Now, click the "Add" button in the middle of the dialog box. The "1" should appear in the "Values to Count" area. Now, click the "Continue" button in this box, and you will be taken back to the "Count Occurrences of Values within Cases" dialog box.

We need to make sure that someone who didn't answer one or more of these six questions—or who didn't answer any of them—is not counted as someone who "disapproves." That would corrupt our data, and the results from this analysis would not be valid. We can prevent this by using a conditional filter: Click the "If" button, and the following dialog box will appear.

First, select the radio button at the top of the box that corresponds to "Include if case satisfies condition." Next we will prepare the condition. Select "Missing Values" from the "Function group" on the right side of the box. Now, choose "Nvalid" from the list of "Functions and Special Variables." Click the arrow to send it to the box under "Include if case satisfies condition." Then in the column on the left, find all six variables having to do with opinions about abortion (abdefect, abhlth, abnomore, abpoor, abrape, and absingle), and drag them between the parentheses next to "NVALID," each separated by a comma. This will return a count for each variable that has a valid response. Therefore, if the value returned is a "6," that means that all six variables contained valid responses for that case. We want all six items to have valid responses; otherwise our new variable might include truncated values (e.g., if someone answered only three questions and approved on all three, the new variable would make it look like he or she approved of only three out of six, or half, when the respondent actually approved in all cases for which he or she replied). So, set this expression equal to six, as displayed in the illustration above.

Now click "Continue" and then the "OK" button in the prior dialog box, to which you will be returned after this one closes. Other than a record of the SPSS/PASW commands executed, no output will be generated. A new variable, however, will be created. See the following screen image for the data contained within the new variable that has been created.

Note that the values, except for those with 0 as the actual value, are all appended with ".00." You will want to go back to the Variable View tab of the Data Editor screen to clean up the details, such as width, decimals, and measure.

Computing an Index Using the Mean

It is possible to construct an index using the "Compute" command in SPSS/PASW Statistics. The most direct way of doing this is to use the "Mean" function. To use this method, click these menus:

TRANSFORM → COMPUTE VARIABLE . . .

When presented with the "Compute Variable" dialog box, select "Mean" from the "Functions and Special Variables" list in the lower right corner. If you don't see "Mean," make sure "Function group," in the area above, is set to "All." After you select "Mean," click the up-arrow, which will send "Mean" to the pane under "Numeric Expression." It will appear as it does in the preceding image. You must then insert all of the variables of interest within the parentheses after "MEAN" (replacing the question marks), each separated by a comma. See the following dialog box for how this is done in the current example:

After selecting the variables from the bank on the left and dragging them into the parentheses, enter the name of the target variable (new variable to be created, in this case, "abscale") in the pane under "Target Variable." Then click the "Type & Label" button. The following short dialog box will be provided:

Click the radio button next to "Label," and enter the appropriate variable label in the adjacent slot. Now, click "Continue," and then "OK." A new variable, "abscale," will be created and appear in the SPSS/PASW Statistics Data Editor window as shown below.

	toldrel3	where12	where8	age2	abopinion	abscale	var	var	var	var
1	0	0	0	0						
2	0	0	0	0	3	1.50				
3	0	0	0	0						
4	0	0	0	0	4	1.33				
5	0	0	0	0	5	1.17				
6	0	0	0	0	1					
7	0	0	0	0	0	2.00				
8	0	0	0	0	0					
9	0	0	0	0		1.00				
10	0	0	0	1	0	2.00				
11	0	0	0	1						
12	0	0	0	0	6	1.00				
13	2	0	0	1	6	1.00				
14	0	0	0	1	6	1.00				
15	0	0	0	0	6	1.00				
16	0	0	0	0		1.50				
17	0	0	0	0	4	1.33				
18	0	0	0	0						
19	0	0	0	0		1.00				
20	0	0	0	0	4	1.33				
21	0	0	0	1		1.00				
22	0	0	0	1	3	1.50				
23	0	0	0	1	3	1.50				
24	0	0	0	1		1.60				
25	0	0	0	1	1	1.83				
26	0	0	0	0	3	1.50				
27	0	0	0	0		1.80				

Data View   Variable View

PASW Statistics Processor is ready

In this case for nonmissing data, notice that the value computed for the mean for each subject falls between (and including) 1 and 2. This is because 1 represents "yes" and 2 represents "no." For statistical purposes, it is sometimes beneficial to have a result between 0 and 1 instead. To arrange for this, you could add a command to subtract the number 1 from the completed mean function in the original "Compute Variable" box, or you can go back now and make the change, as is exhibited as follows. Again, click these menus:

TRANSFORM → COMPUTE VARIABLE . . .

If the dialog box presented is populated with data, click the "Reset" button at the bottom of the box. Now, enter a name for the new variable. (While it is not recommended, you could overwrite the original variable name.) Drag the original variable from the bank on the left to the "Numeric Expression" area. Then, on the calculator-style keypad, click "−" and then "1." This will subtract one from each case and move the data means into the desired range, between 0 and 1, as they are in the following screen image.

Multiple Response

To produce multiple response values (e.g., frequency values combined across multiple variables), choose the following menus:

ANALYZE → MULTIPLE RESPONSE → DEFINE SETS . . .

From the variable bank on the left, move all of the desired variables into the "Variables in Set" box. In this example, the variables chosen are dichotomies, and we are counting the "yes" value, 1. It is also possible to select a category and range. Now, name the set, and type the name in the "Name" slot. You also have the opportunity to place a label at this time, as well. Finally, click the "Add" button on the right side of the dialog box. You can now click "Close."

In order to produce a frequency table for the response set that has just been identified, click the following menus:

ANALYZE → MULTIPLE RESPONSE → FREQUENCIES . . .

Select the response set from the list on the left. (In this case it was the only item in the list.) Move the set to the "Table(s) for" box. Then, click "OK." SPSS/PASW Statistics will produce output like the following:

Case Summary

	\multicolumn{6}{c}{Cases}					
	Valid		Missing		Total	
	N	Percent	N	Percent	N	Percent
$ab^a	1204	59.5%	819	40.5%	2023	100.0%

a. Dichotomy group tabulated at value 1.

$ab Frequencies

		Responses		Percent of Cases
		N	Percent	
$ab[a]	abdefect STRONG CHANCE OF SERIOUS DEFECT	952	20.0%	79.1%
	abhlth WOMANS HEALTH SERIOUSLY ENDANGERED	1146	24.1%	95.2%
	abnomore MARRIED-- WANTS NO MORE CHILDREN	579	12.2%	48.1%
	abpoor LOW INCOME-- CANT AFFORD MORE CHILDREN	556	11.7%	46.2%
	abrape PREGNANT AS RESULT OF RAPE	982	20.7%	81.6%
	absingle NOT MARRIED	536	11.3%	44.5%
Total		4751	100.0%	394.6%

a. Dichotomy group tabulated at value 1.

Note that the multiple response command allows easy production of a table combining similar style variables counting a particular category or range. Above, it is easy to see the similarities and differences in percentages of those who support abortion in the listed circumstances. This frequency table yields the percent of respondents (here called "Percent of Cases") who approve of abortion in the particular case described. Note that 95.2% approve when a woman's health is seriously endangered, while only 44.5% approve when the reason is that a woman is not married.

3

Selecting and
Sampling Cases

S PSS/PASW Statistics software allows a user to draw a sample or sub-sample from a dataset. This selection can be performed to take a random or a targeted sample.

Targeted Selection

For a particular analysis, researchers may not be interested in including all of the cases from a particular data file. There are numerous reasons for this. For instance, if you are interested in studying only characteristics of persons over 21 years of age, then you will need to eliminate any cases in the dataset of individuals who are 21 years of age or under.

This condition comes up most often when using a secondary dataset, one created by a third party, such as the GSS (General Social Survey). Since the dataset was not originally custom tailored to meet your needs, you will need to select the appropriate cases (as well as possibly recode variables, etc., as explained in Chapter 2: Transforming Variables).

To begin, select the following menus:

DATA → SELECT CASES . . .

After choosing those menus, you will be given the "Select Cases" dialog box, as pictured above. Here, you can choose the types of respondents you would like to analyze, and hence ignore those who do not fit your criteria for inclusion. To do so, choose the radio button next to "If condition is satisfied," and then click on the button labeled "If. . ." underneath it. Once you do that, you will be presented with the "Select Cases: If" dialog box, like the one that follows:

The functions in this box are similar in nature and operation to the functions in the "Compute" dialog box used to compute new variables from existing data, which was described in Chapter 1. Suppose, as described earlier, that you wish to include data only from those respondents who were 21 years of age and older.

First, select the necessary variable(s) from the variable bank on the left. In this case, we need the variable "age." Click the arrow to move it to the right side of the dialog box. Now, click the " > = " (greater than or equals) sign, and then enter the number 21. Alternatively you could have selected the ">" (greater than) button and entered the number 20. Since age is measured in whole years in the GSS, in this instance these two methods will both return the same outcome.

Click the "Continue" button in the "Select Cases: If" dialog box, and then click "OK" in the "Select Cases" dialog box. Next, see the Data View window of your dataset:

	relig	age	cohort	finalter	hhrace	phone	racecen1	savesoul	partyid	relneg	c
82	1	50	1958	3	1	3	1	1	2	2	
83	1	50	1958	1	2	3	2	2	0	2	
84	1	19	1989	3	2	3	2	1	0	1	
85	1	60	1948	2	5	3	16	2	1	1	
86	2	51	1957	3	1	3	1	2	3	1	
87	2	70	1938	1	1	3	1	2	4	2	
88	2	40	1968	3	1	6	1	2	2	2	
89	4	54	1954	1	1	3	1	2	1	2	
90	2	43	1965	1	1	3	1	2	6	2	
91	1	33	1975	3	1	3	1	2	5	2	
92	2	63	1945	3	1	3	1	2	1	2	
93	2	60	1948	3	1	3	1	2	2	1	
94	3	57	1951	2	1	3	1	2	1	2	
95	4	29	1979	2	1	3	1	2	4	2	
96	6	57	1951	2	1	3	1	2	1	2	
97	4	48	1960	3	1	3	1	2	0	2	
98	4	27	1981	2	5	3	16	2	3	2	
99	2	89	1919	3	1	3	1	1	9	1	
100	1	44	1964	1	1	3	1	2	5	1	
101	1	63	1945	1	1	3	1	2	5	2	
102	2	99	9999	2	1	2	1	2	9	2	
103	2	35	1973	2	1	3	1	2	1	1	
104	1	19	1989	3	1	3	1	2	2	1	
105	2	83	1925	3	1	3	1	2	1	2	
106	2	76	1932	3	1	3	1	2	6	2	
107	2	21	1987	3	5	6	98	2	3	2	
108	2	41	1967	1	5	3	1	2	1	1	

Note that some of the cases have a diagonal line through the SPSS/PASW Statistics case number at the left. This is how SPSS/PASW Statistics lets you know which cases will be omitted from any and all analyses performed, until the "Select Cases" function is changed or turned off. To turn it off, simply revisit the DATA → SELECT CASES dialog box, and either select "All cases" or click the "Reset" button"; then click "OK."

In the above example, all cases through #83 were included, so to see which ones were omitted, it was necessary to scroll down (as above). Also, note that whenever a case selection is in effect, SPSS/PASW Statistics will alert you with a notification in the lower right hand corner of the screen, indicating "Filter On."

Random Selection

Now, suppose you want to select a random group of cases from a particular dataset. This can also be done by calling up the "Select Cases" dialog box:

DATA → SELECT CASES . . .

This time, click the "Sample" button after choosing the corresponding radio button "Random sample of cases" in the "Select" section of the dialog box. You will then be given the "Select Cases: Random Sample" dialog box.

For this example, 10% of the cases will be chosen. SPSS/PASW Statistics uses the word *approximately*, since not all datasets are necessarily divisible by the percentage that you choose, and hence would not return a whole number of cases in the sample. Note that alternatively, you could select the other radio button and choose an exact number of cases from the first *N* number of cases, as the file is sorted. (Use the DATA → SORT CASES menu to change the way the cases in your dataset are ordered in SPSS/PASW Statistics.)

Click "Continue"; then click "OK" when you are taken back to the "Select Cases" dialog box. The image below shows the Variable View tab in the Data Editor window after this action was performed.

	ballot	born	dateintv	famgen	family16	form	formwt	hompop	id	inthisp	is
1	2	1	503	2	1	1	1.000	2	1	1	
2	1	2	427	1	5	1	1.000	1	2	1	
3	2	1	717	1	5	1	1.000	2	3	1	
4	3	1	519	2	5	1	1.000	3	4	1	
5	1	2	630	2	8	1	1.000	3	5	1	
6	2	1	617	1	1	1	1.000	2	6	1	
7	3	2	611	2	1	1	1.000	5	7	1	
8	2	2	717	2	1	1	1.000	5	8	1	
9	1	2	624	1	1	1	1.000	1	9	1	
10	3	2	821	1	1	1	1.000	1	10	1	
11	2	1	426	1	3	1	1.000	2	11	1	
12	3	2	526	1	1	1	1.000	1	12	1	
13	3	1	626	2	1	1	1.000	2	13	1	
14	3	1	504	1	1	1	1.000	2	14	1	
15	3	1	627	1	1	1	1.000	1	15	1	
16	1	2	507	2	1	1	1.000	6	16	1	
17	1	2	612	1	1	1	1.000	2	17	1	
18	2	1	507	2	1	1	1.000	6	18	1	
19	3	2	518	1	1	1	1.000	1	19	1	
20	1	2	512	2	1	1	1.000	4	20	1	
21	3	1	820	1	1	1	1.000	2	21	1	
22	3	2	522	5	1	2	1.000	3	22	1	
23	3	1	508	1	4	2	1.000	2	23	1	
24	1	1	616	4	1	2	1.000	4	24	1	
25	3	1	611	1	1	2	1.000	1	25	1	
26	3	1	623	2	1	2	1.000	4	26	1	
27	3	2	905	1	5	2	1.000	2	27	1	

Many (approximately 90%) of the cases have a diagonal line through the SPSS/PASW Statistics case number at the left. Again, this is how SPSS/PASW Statistics lets you know which cases will be omitted from any and all analyses performed, until the "Select Cases" function is changed or turned off. Note that the "Filter On" alert in the lower right hand corner of the Data Editor window reminds you that only a subsample of the dataset will be used for any and all analyses requested.

Selecting Cases for Inclusion in a New Dataset

Up to this point, we have selected cases from a dataset while having SPSS/PASW Statistics ignore those cases that were not selected for inclusion. It is also possible to have SPSS/PASW Statistics create a new data file that contains only the cases that have been selected.

The process of case selection is identical. The difference is in the "Output" section of the dialog box:

DATA → SELECT CASES . . .

Choose the radio button for "Copy selected cases to a new dataset." Then enter a name for your new file; here the name is "newsample." The file will be stored in the default directory as an SPSS/PASW Statistics *.sav file. The advantage to choosing this option is that you can work with the subset data file without risk of altering the full original data file. The resulting Data Editor window is shown below.

	ballot	born	dateintv	famgen	family16	form	formwt	hompop	id	inthisp	is
1	1	2	624	1	1	1	1.000	1	9	1	
2	3	2	526	1	1	1	1.000	1	12	1	
3	1	2	512	2	1	1	1.000	4	20	1	
4	3	2	424	1	5	2	1.000	1	29	1	
5	1	2	821	2	1	2	1.000	3	32	1	
6	1	2	520	1	1	1	1.000	1	34	4	
7	3	2	520	1	5	1	1.000	2	43	1	
8	2	1	831	2	1	2	1.000	4	60	1	
9	3	1	421	2	5	2	1.000	3	70	1	
10	3	1	608	2	1	1	1.000	2	72	1	
11	1	1	523	2	1	1	1.000	3	79	1	
12	1	1	522	2	3	2	1.000	4	97	1	
13	3	1	514	2	1	2	1.000	3	117	1	
14	2	1	509	6	1	1	1.000	5	126	2	
15	3	1	603	1	1	1	1.000	2	138	1	
16	3	1	817	2	4	2	1.000	7	145	1	
17	2	2	820	1	1	2	1.000	2	146	1	
18	3	2	602	6	8	1	1.000	4	156	1	
19	3	2	621	2	1	1	1.000	4	159	30	
20	2	1	808	1	1	1	1.000	1	171	1	
21	1	1	522	1	1	2	1.000	2	173	2	
22	2	2	517	1	5	2	1.000	3	174	2	
23	2	1	519	1	5	2	1.000	1	175	1	
24	2	1	628	1	1	2	1.000	1	178	30	
25	2	1	620	2	1	2	1.000	3	179	30	
26	1	1	807	2	5	2	1.000	3	180	1	
27	3	1	708	2	1	2	1.000	4	181	1	

Note that the file has already been assigned the name, "newsample," that you provided in the "Select Cases" dialog box; the name appears at the top of the Data Editor window. Also, pay special attention to the variable "id." Since the GSS maintains the "id" variable, you will always be able to track case numbers in the event that you sort cases in a different order. In this instance, you will know which cases were randomly selected from the original GSS dataset for this subsample by looking at the "id" variable.

4

Organization and Presentation of Information

In this chapter, basic methods of data description will be exhibited. This information will include frequency distributions, measures of central tendency, and measures of variability. Presentation can be made in the form of a table, chart, or graph.

Measures of Central Tendency and Variability

In order to quickly produce a table with basic descriptive statistics about a variable or variables, select the following menus:

ANALYZE → DESCRIPTIVE STATISTICS → DESCRIPTIVES . . .

By clicking on the "Options" button at the upper right hand corner of the "Descriptives" dialog box, you will open another dialog box that will allow you to choose which basic descriptive information will be produced by SPSS/PASW Statistics.

Leave a check mark in the box next to those statistics that you would like to request. You also have the option of choosing the display order; choose one of the four options. After clicking "Continue" in this dialog box and "OK" in the original one, you will be given the following SPSS/PASW Statistics output:

Descriptive Statistics

	N	Minimum	Maximum	Mean	Std. Deviation
age AGE OF RESPONDENT	2013	18	89	47.71	17.351
sei RESPONDENT SOCIOECONOMIC INDEX	1911	17.1	97.2	48.760	19.5061
tvhours HOURS PER DAY WATCHING TV	1324	0	24	2.98	2.659
Valid N (listwise)	1248				

Note that the sample sizes along with the four measures that were selected for each variable have been presented in separate columns. Variables are listed in the rows of the table output.

While this method of getting basic descriptive information is very quick and easy, it is possible to get more detailed descriptive information about variables in a dataset. Note, for instance, that the previous method will NOT allow you to obtain the median. You can obtain information about measures of central tendency (including the median) and variability, and you can obtain actual frequency distribution tables.

Frequency Distributions

Using the same variables as in the previous example, select the following menus:

ANALYZE → DESCRIPTIVE STATISTICS → FREQUENCIES . . .

The three selected variables, "age," "sei," and "tvhours," are all scale variables. Therefore, frequency distribution tables for these variables would have too many categories and be too long to be of any real use. You must be cognizant of the level of measurement and categorization of variables before selecting tables. Therefore, make sure that the "Display frequency tables" box is *unchecked*. After removing the check mark, you will be presented with a pop-up box like this one:

Click "OK" to return to the "Frequencies" dialog box.

To choose which statistical information to request, click the "Statistics" button in the upper right corner of the "Frequencies" dialog box, and you will be presented with the following new dialog box.

Here, you can choose measures of central tendency (mean, median, and/or mode) and measures of variability. Quartiles are useful for computing the interquartile range (IQR). You can also select any percentile for computation as well, depending on your specific needs. Based on the above dialog boxes, the following output will be provided once you click "Continue" and then "OK" in the original dialog box:

Statistics

		age AGE OF RESPONDENT	sei RESPONDENT SOCIOECONOMIC INDEX	tvhours HOURS PER DAY WATCHING TV
N	Valid	2013	1911	1324
	Missing	10	112	699
Mean		47.71	48.760	2.98
Median		47.00	39.000	2.00
Mode		50	63.5	2
Std. Deviation		17.351	19.5061	2.659
Variance		301.052	380.487	7.071
Range		71	80.1	24
Minimum		18	17.1	0
Maximum		89	97.2	24
Percentiles	25	34.00	32.300	1.00
	50	47.00	39.000	2.00
	75	60.00	63.500	4.00

Now, perform the same menu function with a different variable:

ANALYZE → DESCRIPTIVES → FREQUENCIES . . .

First, remove the variables that were there by using the arrow to send them back to the variable list or by clicking the "Reset" button. Note that if you click the "Reset" button, entries made in the "Statistics" portion of this box will also revert to default, so you would need to click the "Statistics" button and select the appropriate statistics.

Now, select "age2," the recoded age dichotomy variable (we created this variable in Chapter 2: Transforming Variables), and drag it into the "Variable(s)" area. Click the "Charts" button. You will be given a subdialog box as follows.

Choose the "Pie charts" radio button and "Frequencies." (Of course, depending on your needs, and the level of measurement of your variable[s], you could select any of these types of charts.) Then click "Continue" and then "OK" in the original dialog box. The information below represents the output that SPSS/PASW Statistics will provide:

Statistics

age2 Age 50 & over, or not

N	Valid	2013
	Missing	10
Mean		.45
Median		.00
Mode		0
Std. Deviation		.497
Variance		.247
Range		1
Minimum		0
Maximum		1
Percentiles	25	.00
	50	.00
	75	1.00

age2 Age 50 & over, or not

		Frequency	Percent	Valid Percent	Cumulative Percent
Valid	0 Aged 49 or less	1113	55.0	55.3	55.3
	1 Aged 50 or more	900	44.5	44.7	100.0
	Total	2013	99.5	100.0	
Missing	System	10	.5		
Total		2023	100.0		

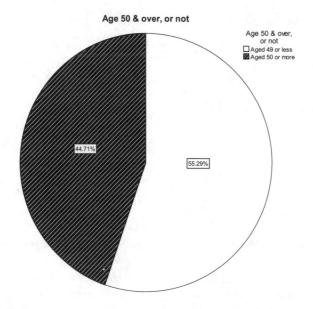

Age 50 & over, or not

While this is one way to obtain some of the chart and graph options, there are more detailed options and optimized interfaces to produce charts and graphs that are explained in the next chapter. Your chart will likely appear in color and without data labels (percentages in each slice). Instructions for using these features are also addressed in Chapter 5: Charts and Graphs.

Now, suppose that you want to produce a frequency distribution for respondent's age beyond just the dichotomy that was demonstrated in the previous example. It is not feasible to run the frequency command and use its menus using the variable "age," since a virtually useless table listing all ages in the data file would be generated.

In order to present a useful frequency distribution, it makes sense to divide the interval-ratio variable, "age," into meaningful or otherwise appropriate categories. Take, for instance, the following example, where "age" is divided into ranges according to decade. Bear in mind that the GSS contains responses only from noninstitutionalized Americans 18 years of age and above. First, use the following menus to recode age into "agegroup" (see Chapter 2 for more details on recoding):

TRANSFORM → RECODE INTO DIFFERENT VARIABLES . . .

Select the original variable from the variable list on the left, and drag it into the "Numeric Variable –> Output Variable" area. On the right side of the dialog box, name the new variable (here, the new name is "agegroup"), and provide a label if desired. Be sure to click the "Change" button after to assign the new name that you have entered. Now, click the "Old and New Values" button. The following dialog box will be presented:

Here, enter the old values and ranges on the left in conjunction with the new value on the right, clicking the "Add" button after each pair of entries. For more details, review the recoding section of Chapter 2: Transforming Variables. After all of the old and new value changes have been added to the list, click the "Continue" button in this window and then the "OK" button in the "Recode Into Different Variables" dialog box. The new variable will be displayed in the SPSS/PASW Statistics Data Editor window.

Click the Variable View tab and find the newly created variable. Since there are no decimals, change that to "0." Also, there will be no values with more than one digit, so change the width to "1." By recoding the variable, we have transformed it from a scale (ratio) variable into an ordinal variable, so select "ordinal" in the Measure column for the new "agegroup" variable. In the "Values" cell, click the button with three dots. You will be given the following dialog box:

Enter the appropriate labels, as done in the example above. Then click "OK." This will record the value labels onto the variable.

Next, request a frequency distribution for the newly structured variable. To do so, click the following menus:

ANALYZE → DESCRIPTIVE STATISTICS → FREQUENCIES . . .

When given the above dialog box, drag the variable of interest from the list on the left into the "Variable(s)" area. For a visual representation of the distribution, select the "Charts . . ." button, and see the dialog box that follows:

Click the radio button next to "Histograms," and check the box for "Show normal curve on histogram." This will produce a histogram with an overlay of a normal curve for reference. Click the "Continue" button here, and then click "OK" in the prior dialog box. SPSS/PASW Statistics will generate the following output, consisting of an easy-to-understand frequency table and a histogram.

agegroup: "Age by groups"

		Frequency	Percent	Valid Percent	Cumulative Percent
Valid	1 18-19	37	1.8	1.8	1.8
	2 20-29	322	15.9	16.0	17.8
	3 30-39	373	18.4	18.5	36.4
	4 40-49	381	18.8	18.9	55.3
	5 50-59	371	18.3	18.4	73.7
	6 60-69	272	13.4	13.5	87.2
	7 70-79	165	8.2	8.2	95.4
	8 80-89	92	4.5	4.6	100.0
	Total	2013	99.5	100.0	
Missing	System	10	.5		
Total		2023	100.0		

Note that by inspecting the "Valid Percent" column, one can readily get a sense of the distribution, due to the manageable number of categories (rows) in the table. This same information is provided graphically in the histogram that follows:

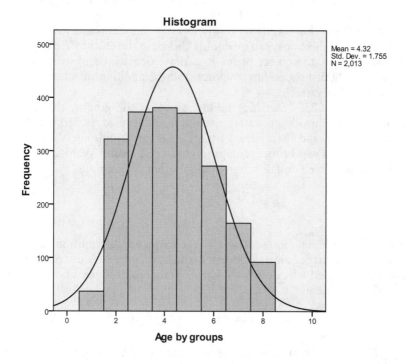

Histogram

5

Charts and Graphs

In this chapter, the techniques for producing a number of useful graphics will be explained. There are a number of other chart and graph options that are not explained in this section, though they are contained within the "Graphs" menu and can be explored with knowledge of how to use the other SPSS/PASW Statistics graph functions along with a background in statistical and research methods.

Most of the charts and graphs discussed in this section, as well as those not covered in this book, can be double clicked in the Output Viewer. After double-clicking, the object opens in a new "Chart Editor" window that allows editing of text, colors, graphics, and the addition of other features and even other variables.

From the SPSS "Statistics Editor" window, the graphs, charts, and tables that are produced can be selected and copied (<Ctrl> + C or <Apple> + C), and then pasted (<Ctrl> + V or <Apple> + V, or "Paste Special") into a word processing program like Microsoft Word, a publishing program, a web design program, or another program.

Boxplot

A boxplot is a visual representation of the frequency distribution of a variable showing shape, central tendency, and variability of a distribution. It can also be called a box-and-whisker diagram. To produce a boxplot, use the "Graphs" menu:

GRAPHS → CHART BUILDER . . .

If this is the first time you've used the SPSS/PASW Statistics "Chart Builder," then you may receive the following alert box.

This alert is an important reminder of at least two things. First, it is important to define the proper of level of measurement for any variables for which you will be using this function. Scale (interval and ratio) variables should not be used, for instance, to produce a pie chart. The "Chart Builder" will actually not allow some improper graphing and charting. So, it is doubly important to properly assign levels of measurement in any dataset you use, whether it is a secondary dataset or whether you collect and enter the data yourself.

Also, make certain that value labels have been assigned properly for nominal and ordinal variables. Without those labels, it may not be possible to make proper use of the information provided by the SPSS/PASW Statistics "Chart Builder."

In this example, we will draw a simple boxplot for one variable, "age." From the "Chart Builder" dialog box (see above), select "Boxplot" from the Gallery at the bottom of this window. SPSS/PASW Statistics presents three choices for the boxplot. For this example, we will select the third choice, examining just one variable. Drag and drop the icon for your selection into the chart preview area toward the top right side of this window. An area marked "X-Axis?" will appear along the left-hand side of the chart preview pane.

Now, you will need to select a variable from the list on the left to drag into this "X-Axis?" area. SPSS/PASW Statistics requires a variable to be dragged to that area in order to compute and draw the boxplot. Once you do this, the screen will look like the one below:

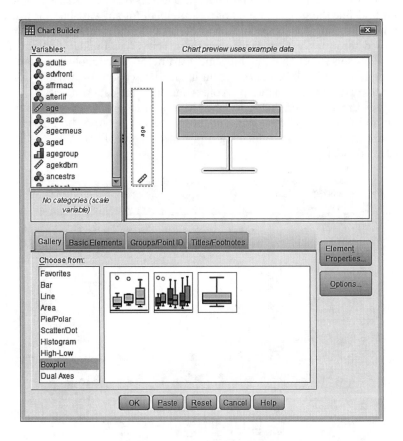

The "Element Properties" window will automatically open. Here, you have options to set the scale range for the graph, as well as the label for the X-Axis in this case. (Labels, titles, legends, and so on, can all be edited in the output window of SPSS/PASW Statistics, as well; see Chapter 11: Editing Output.)

Once you have set your preferences, click "OK" in the "Chart Builder" dialog box, and SPSS/PASW Statistics will produce the boxplot in the Output Viewer window. Information about the distribution of the variable is contained in the boxplot. The upper and lower boundaries of the box itself represent Q3 (the 75th percentile) and Q1 (the 25th percentile), respectively. Values correspond to the scale on the left axis of the figure. Therefore, the box itself shows the IQR (interquartile range). The line inside the box is drawn at the 50th percentile (median). The lines extending above and below the box are referred to as whiskers. At the end of the top whisker, the maximum score is marked. The minimum value can be found at the end of the lower whisker.

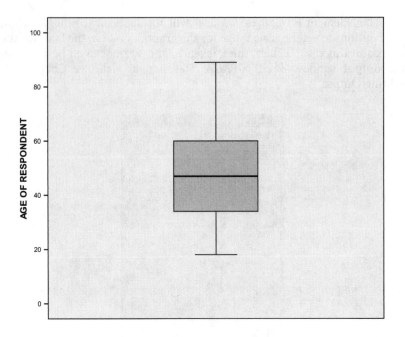

Legacy Options for Graphs (Boxplot Example)

The "Chart Builder" is a newer feature in SPSS/PASW Statistics. The option to create charts and graphs using the previous system remains in the program and can be particularly useful for quick creation of certain output, if the researcher knows exactly what type of visual display is desired in advance:

GRAPHS → LEGACY DIALOGS → BOXPLOT . . .

In this example, we will draw a simple boxplot for one variable, "age," as we did before with the "Chart Builder." Click "Simple," and select the button for "Summaries of separate variables." Then click the "Define" button. You will be given another dialog box:

In this dialog box, drag the variable(s) of interest into the "Boxes Represent" location. Click "OK," and SPSS/PASW Statistics will provide the boxplot(s) that you have requested. It will be nearly identical to the output provided by the Chart Builder option, varying only in ways related to additional formatting options that are selected using the "Chart Builder."

Scatterplot

A scatterplot is a useful graph to display the relationship between two scale, or interval-ratio, variables. To create a scatterplot, use these menu directions:

GRAPHS → CHART BUILDER . . .

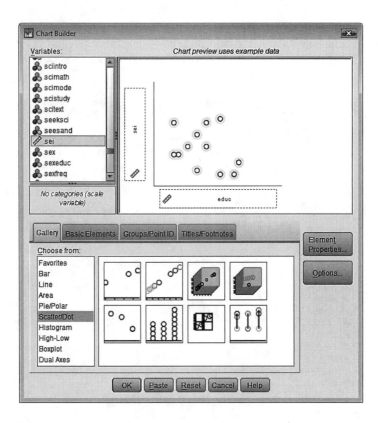

In the "Chart Builder" window, select "Scatter/Dot" from the Gallery. Drag and drop the type of scatterplot you would like to produce into the chart preview area. For this example, choose the first option and drag it to the preview area. Once it is there, you will need to select variables for both the X and Y axes. For this example, we will plot socioeconomic index by years of education. Drag the "sei" variable from the "Variables" bank on the left into the Y-Axis location. Then drag the "educ" variable from the "Variables" bank into the X-Axis location. Make certain that the levels of measurement for both "sei" and "educ" have been recorded as "scale" (interval-ratio). You can use the "Element Properties" window to change the scale of the graph, edit labels, and so on.

Click "OK" in the "Chart Builder," and SPSS will provide the scatter-plot in the Output Viewer window, as illustrated below. In the graph for SEI by Years of Education, there does appear to be an upward trend. Note also that the data points all fall along vertical lines due to the nature of the variable "educ," which has been categorized into discrete numbers of years (not allowing for 13.5 years, for instance). In the case of a true continuously measured variable, those distinct vertical lines would not show up in the scatterplot.

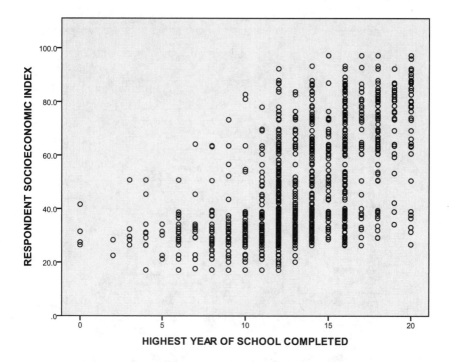

Legacy Scatterplot

To utilize the legacy option, the method still available from prior versions of SPSS software, for creating a scatterplot, use the following menus, and proceed using the same information that was entered using the "Chart Builder" option:

GRAPHS → LEGACY DIALOGS → SCATTER/DOT . . .

Then, click "Simple Scatter" for our example. (Note that there are several other types of scatterplots available to you, depending upon the nature of the variables you wish to graph.) Click "Define." You will then be presented with the "Simple Scatterplot" dialog box like the one following.

Select variables for the X and Y axes. In this example, "sei" (socioeconomic status) has been selected for the Y-Axis (dependent variable), and "edu" (years of education) has been chosen for the X-Axis (independent variable). Once you click the "OK" button, SPSS/PASW Statistics will produce a scatterplot nearly identical to the one provided using the "Chart Builder" option.

Histogram

In order to display a graphic representation of the distribution of a single scale variable, the histogram serves well. This is a bar graph that can be used with variables at the interval and ratio levels. The bars touch. The width of the bars represents the width of the intervals, and the height of the bars represents the frequency of each interval. To create a histogram, follow these menus:

GRAPHS → CHART BUILDER . . .

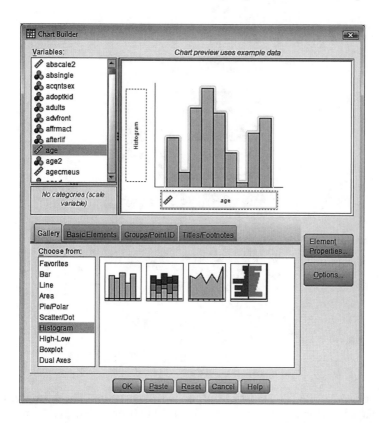

In the "Chart Builder" dialog box, select "Histogram" from the Gallery at the bottom of the window. Then choose the appropriate option; in this example, we will use the first option. Now, drag the variable of interest into the chart preview area. In this case, "age" is the variable selected.

Next, in the "Element Properties" window, making sure that you are editing properties of "Bar1," check the box that is associated with "Display normal curve." Then, click "Apply" in the "Element Properties" window and click "OK" in the "Chart Builder" box.

The SPSS/PASW Statistics output is shown below. The histogram is displayed, and an overlay of a normal curve has been added, per the request we made in the "Element Properties" window.

Multivariate Histogram

To produce a stacked histogram, displaying stacked bars of one variable's distribution according to categories of another variable, select the second histogram option in the "Chart Builder" dialog box, the one in which each bar has several different colors. Add the variable of interest, "age," to the X-Axis. Then, drag the variable by which you would like the bars divided into the "Stack: set color" box, which will appear in the chart preview area when you drag "age" into it.

Note that you cannot divide bars by a variable that is "scale" according to SPSS/PASW Statistics. Even if it is a nominal variable, you cannot move it to the "Stack" area in the chart preview pane unless SPSS/PASW Statistics recognizes it as nominal or ordinal. To change a variable from scale to nominal or ordinal (assuming it is indeed not a scale variable), go to the Variable View tab of the Data Editor window. Find the variable you wish to change, click on its cell in the "Measure" column, and then select the new level of measurement from the pull down choices: nominal, ordinal, or scale.

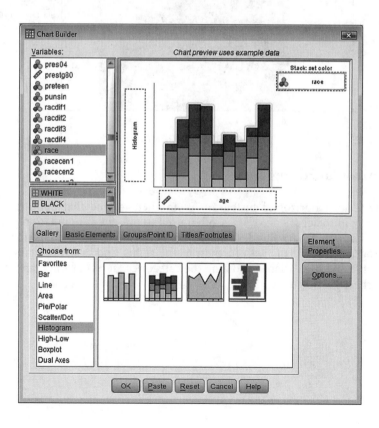

Click "OK," and the following output will be produced in the SPSS/
PASW Statistics Output Viewer:

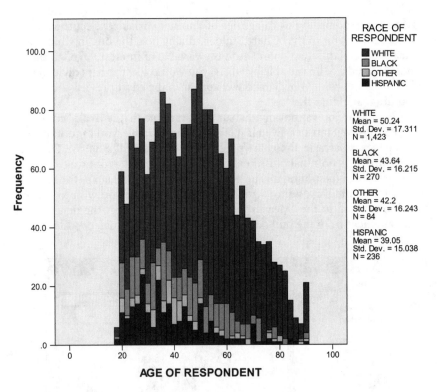

Horizontal Histogram

A two-sided horizontal histogram is another graphic that appears frequently in social science classes, often used to present a "population pyra-
mid." In the "Chart Builder" dialog box, click the fourth choice for the
histogram option (the icon furthest to the right), and drag the main axis
variable and the variable to define the categories (sides) of the graph into
the chart preview area.

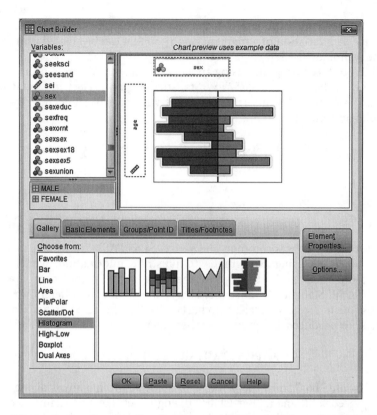

If you use "age" as the distribution variable and wish to divide the distribution by "sex," the following output will be returned after you click "OK":

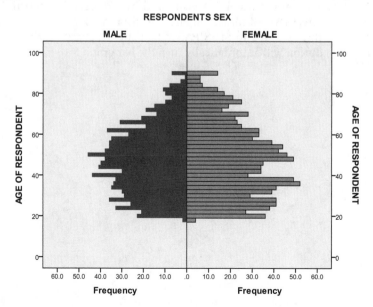

Note that the third option in the histogram Gallery area of the "Chart Builder" is a variation of a frequency polygon that can be created using the same technique used to create the first histogram option.

To produce histograms using an older version of SPSS, or to utilize that method in the newer SPSS/PASW Statistics versions, select the following menus, and enter the information about your variables and the type of graph you would like to produce:

GRAPHS → LEGACY DIALOGS → HISTOGRAM . . .

Bar Graph

Usage of bar graphs is common and varied. SPSS/PASW Statistics provides many ways of using bar graphs to illustrate information. Much like Microsoft Excel and other spreadsheet and data graphics programs, SPSS/PASW Statistics produces bar charts in a number of different ways. It is possible to create standard bar charts as well as clustered or stacked bar charts. To produce a bar graph, use these menus:

GRAPHS → CHART BUILDER . . .

Choose "Bar" from the Gallery. You will be given a small dialog box that precedes the main "Bar Chart" dialog boxes. For this example, click "Simple," and then click the "Define" button. Now you will be given the "Define Simple Bar" dialog box and can enter the information to produce the graph.

Be sure that your variable is recognized by SPSS/PASW Statistics as having the correct level of measurement. For instance, if you have a nominal variable that is coded in SPSS/PASW Statistics as a scale variable, the "Bar" graph option will automatically turn the bar graph into a histogram.

Choose the first bar graph option, and drag it into the chart preview area. Select the variable for graphing from the list on the left, and drag it into the X-Axis box. Then click "OK." Following is an image of the graph that SPSS/PASW Statistics will produce.

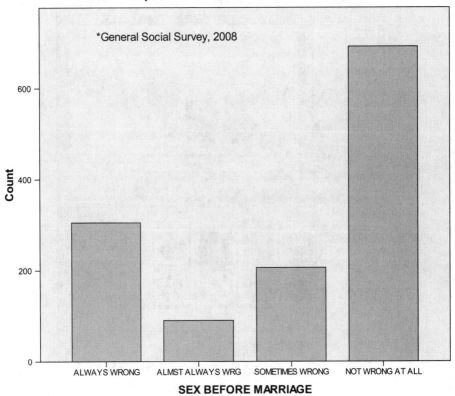

Respondents' Beliefs About Premarital Sex*

*General Social Survey, 2008

Note that a title and annotation have been added. This can be done by, first, double-clicking the graph in the SPSS/PASW Statistics Output Viewer. Then, in the "Chart Editor" dialog box that appears, use the "Option" menu to add a title and/or a text box. The text box can be moved and/or resized. More information about how to add features or edit graphs can be found in Chapter 11: Editing Output.

Multivariate Bar Graph

One might wish to produce clustered bar graphs when comparing information, such as that shown above about beliefs concerning premarital sex, across categories of things like gender, race/ethnicity, or age groups. In the example that follows, we examine beliefs about premarital sex by gender. With a clustered bar graph in this case, it is beneficial to graph the percent of respondents versus the number of respondents, so that the relative bar lengths can be more easily compared within categories of the dependent variable. So, select the following menus:

GRAPHS → CHART BUILDER . . .

After selecting "Bar" from the Gallery, select the clustered option, which is the second icon from the left in the top row, as seen in the following image. Then drag it to the chart preview area.

You have the option at this point to enter titles and footnotes by selecting the Titles/Footnotes tab from the row of tabs to the right of the Gallery tab. In this example, you will notice that the output (shown in the figure below) has been edited to include a title and footnote. (You can also add this information later in the SPSS/PASW Statistics Output Viewer window by double-clicking the object and working with the editing tools there; for more information, see Chapter 11: Editing Output.)

Now, tell SPSS/PASW Statistics with which variables you will be working. Drag the dependent variable, "premarsx," into the X-Axis box in the chart preview area. Next, drag the independent variable, "sex," from the variable list into the "Cluster on X" box in the chart preview area.

Next, select "Element Properties" and make sure to change the bar graph option from count to percentage.

Then click on the "Set Parameters" button, and elect the option for percentage that uses all of the bars of the same color (total for that grouping category) as the denominator.

Now, click "Continue" in this box, then "Apply" in the Element Properties box, and then "OK" in the "Chart Builder" window. SPSS/PASW Statistics will produce the following output:

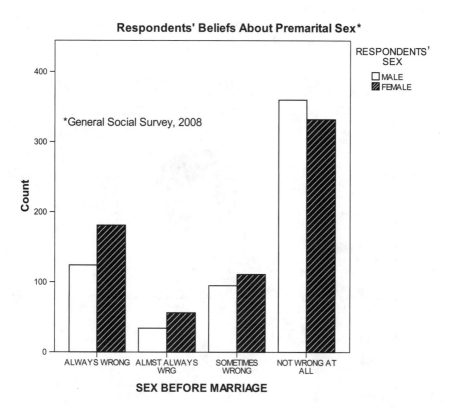

Respondents' Beliefs About Premarital Sex*

It is apparent from the bar chart prepared by SPSS/PASW Statistics that females tend to take a less favorable view of premarital sex than do males. Notice that a larger percentage of women than men in the sample responded "always wrong." Likewise, a smaller percentage of the women responded "not wrong at all."

To produce bar graphs using an older version of SPSS, or to use a legacy method on a newer version of SPSS/PASW Statistics, select the following menus, and enter the information about your variables and the type of graph you would like to produce:

GRAPHS → LEGACY DIALOGS → BAR . . .

Pie Chart

Pie charts are circular graphs with slices that represent the proportion of the total contained within each category. In order to produce a pie chart, select the following menus:

GRAPHS → CHART BUILDER . . .

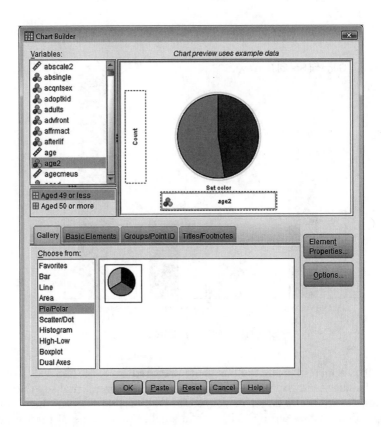

Remember, SPSS/PASW Statistics will not allow you to utilize variables that it recognizes as "scale" to draw a pie chart. If the variable you wish to draw is not scale, you may change the level of measurement recognition for that variable in the Variable View tab of the Data Editor by double-clicking on that variable's cell in the "Measure" column.

For this example, use "age2," the recoded version of respondent's age. "Age2" reduces the data into exactly two categories; this is known as a dichotomy. A pie chart is useful for nominal and many ordinal variables and particularly for dichotomies. It would be of little or no use to create a pie chart for the original "age" variable, since there would be too many slices from which to make much sense.

First click "Pie/Polar" from the Gallery at the bottom of the "Chart Builder" box. Then drag the icon for the only available option to the chart preview area. Now, drag the "age2" variable to the box that appears underneath the sample pie chart in the chart preview area.

Again, note that you have the option here to select the Titles/Footnotes tab, where you will be presented with spaces to easily enter that information. In this example, you will notice that the output (below) has been edited to include a title and footnote. (You can also add this information later in the SPSS/PASW Statistics Output Viewer window by double-clicking the object and working with the editing tools there; for more information, see Chapter 11: Editing Output.)

Next, click on "Element Properties," and choose "Polar interval1."

In the "Statistics" box, select "Percentage." There will be only one choice when you click the "Set Parameters" button: Grand Total.

Now, click the "Continue" button, then the "Apply" button in the "Element Properties" window, and then the "OK" button in the "Chart Builder" box. The following graphic will be produced in the SPSS/PASW Statistics Output Viewer window:

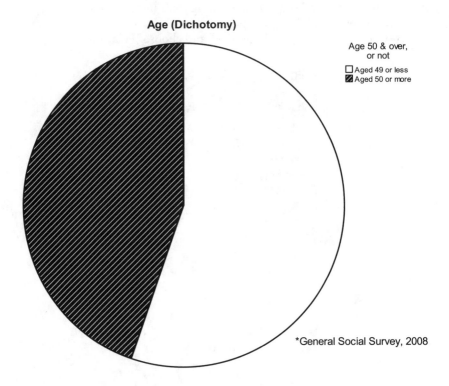

The SPSS/PASW Statistics output above provides descriptive (percentage) information in visual form for the variable selected, "age2": age distribution reduced into two categories.

To produce pie charts using older versions of SPSS Software or its legacy method, select the following menus, and enter the information about your variables and the type of chart you would like to produce:

GRAPHS → LEGACY DIALOGS → PIE . . .

Additional Graphic Capabilities in SPSS/PASW Statistics

Using the SPSS/PASW Statistics "Chart Builder," you can create additional types of graphics not covered in this chapter, such as line graphs and graphs with dual axes, by selecting those templates from the Gallery in the "Chart Builder" box. The options for patterns, clustering, and so on can be followed from the instructions for the graphs discussed in this chapter.

6

Cross-Tabulation and Measures of Association for Nominal and Ordinal Variables

The most basic type of cross-tabulation (crosstabs) is used to analyze relationships between two variables. This allows a researcher to explore the relationship between variables by examining the intersections of categories of each of the variables involved. The simplest type of cross-tabulation is bivariate analysis, an analysis of two variables. However, the analysis can be expanded beyond that.

Bivariate Analysis

Follow these menus to conduct a sample cross-tabulation of two variables:

ANALYZE → DESCRIPTIVE STATISTICS → CROSSTABS . . .

After selecting those menus, you will be presented with a dialog box like the one above. Here, you will have the opportunity to select the row and column variables for the bivariate table. As is customary, it is recommended that you choose the independent variable as the column variable. Above, "cappun" (view on capital punishment/the death penalty) has been selected for the row variable, and "race" (recoded version of respondent's race) has been chosen as the column variable. We use "race," since the number of categories has been limited to four, based on three categories in the original race variable (now "race3") and 50 categories of the variable "Hispanic." It is easier to interpret data from cross-tabulations when the number of categories is kept smaller. Next, click on the "Cells" button to choose options about what information will be given in the output table. The "Crosstabs: Cell Display" dialog box will open.

Be sure that the "Column" box is checked under "Percentages." This will make sure that you have information from the appropriate perspective to analyze your variables based on which is the predictor. Click "Continue" in the "Cell Display" dialog box and then "OK" in the original "Crosstabs" dialog box. The table that follows comes from the output produced by following the aforementioned steps:

cappun FAVOR OR OPPOSE DEATH PENALTY FOR MURDER * race RACE OF RESPONDENT Crosstabulation

			race RACE OF RESPONDENT				Total
			1 WHITE	2 BLACK	3 OTHER	4 HISPANIC	
cappun FAVOR OR OPPOSE DEATH PENALTY FOR MURDER	1 FAVOR	Count	979	111	50	123	1263
		% within race RACE OF RESPONDENT	72.6%	44.4%	66.7%	53.7%	66.4%
	2 OPPOSE	Count	369	139	25	106	639
		% within race RACE OF RESPONDENT	27.4%	55.6%	33.3%	46.3%	33.6%
Total		Count	1348	250	75	229	1902
		% within race RACE OF RESPONDENT	100.0%	100.0%	100.0%	100.0%	100.0%

Based on the information in the table, it is easy to see that there is some sort of relationship between the variables of interest in this case. Note that by looking at the percentages across the columns (categories of the independent variable), you can see that there are differences in opinion about the death penalty by race. According to these GSS data, Whites (72.6%) and Others (66.7%) are more likely to favor the death penalty than Hispanics (53.7%) or Blacks (44.4%).

Adding Another Variable or Dimension to the Analysis

Suppose we want to further explore the bivariate relationship that we briefly examined in the preceding section. By adding another variable, such as respondent's sex, we can further explore how opinions about capital punishment are held in the United States. One way that we can perform this type of analysis is to split our data file by respondent's sex. At that point, any analysis that we do will be performed across the categories of the variable with which we have split the dataset.

In order to split the data file by respondent's sex, use these menus:

DATA → SPLIT FILE . . .

You will be given a "Split File" dialog box like the one above. Here, choose the "Compare groups" radio button. This will brighten the "Groups Based on" box and allow you to drag variables into that box, and these variables will then be used to split the data file. Find "sex" from the variable bank on the left and drag it over into the "Groups Based on" box. It is often a good idea to make sure that the file is sorted by grouping variables, though this is not necessary, by clicking the radio button just below the "Groups Based on" box. To continue, click "OK."

SPSS/PASW Statistics will now perform the split file function. You will know that the data file has been split by the indicator in the lower right hand window of the Data Editor screen. It will say "Split by sex."

Now, go back to the "Crosstabs" box, and perform the same operations that were done in the previous section. (The variables and setting should remain the same from before, so unless you've restarted SPSS/PASW Statistics in between, it will be just a matter of choosing "OK" once the dialog box appears.)

ANALYZE → DESCRIPTIVE STATISTICS → CROSSTABS . . .

cappun FAVOR OR OPPOSE DEATH PENALTY FOR MURDER * race RACE OF RESPONDENT Crosstabulation

sex RESPONDENTS SEX				race RACE OF RESPONDENT				
				1 WHITE	2 BLACK	3 OTHER	4 HISPANIC	Total
1 MALE	cappun FAVOR OR OPPOSE DEATH PENALTY FOR MURDER	1 FAVOR	Count	490	53	27	61	631
			% within race RACE OF RESPONDENT	78.1%	49.5%	65.9%	55.5%	71.3%
		2 OPPOSE	Count	137	54	14	49	254
			% within race RACE OF RESPONDENT	21.9%	50.5%	34.1%	44.5%	28.7%
	Total		Count	627	107	41	110	885
			% within race RACE OF RESPONDENT	100.0%	100.0%	100.0%	100.0%	100.0%
2 FEMALE	cappun FAVOR OR OPPOSE DEATH PENALTY FOR MURDER	1 FAVOR	Count	489	58	23	62	632
			% within race RACE OF RESPONDENT	67.8%	40.6%	67.6%	52.1%	62.1%
		2 OPPOSE	Count	232	85	11	57	385
			% within race RACE OF RESPONDENT	32.2%	59.4%	32.4%	47.9%	37.9%
	Total		Count	721	143	34	119	1017
			% within race RACE OF RESPONDENT	100.0%	100.0%	100.0%	100.0%	100.0%

The preceding table will be presented as part of the output that SPSS/PASW Statistics returns. While it is similar to the table given in the prior section, note that it has twice as many cells. It has been split into two tables, one for males, and one for females. In this instance the table shows, among other things, that Black females have the lowest percentage of all categories of men and women who "favor the death penalty for murder." In all racial categories except "Other," men tended to be more likely to favor the death penalty. By adding this new dimension, we were able to obtain some additional insight into public opinion on this matter. See your statistics or research methods book(s) for more details.

Measures of Association for Nominal and Ordinal Variables

PRE (proportional reduction in error) statistics allow us to determine the proportional reduction of error achieved by adding one or more variables to an analysis (even if it is the initial independent variable). "PRE measures are derived by comparing the errors made in predicting the dependent variable while ignoring the independent variable with errors made when making predictions that use information about the independent variable" (Frankfort-Nachmias & Leon-Guerrero, 2006). For nominal variables, a PRE statistic that we can utilize is *lambda*. For details on how lambda is specifically calculated, see Chapter 12 of *Social Statistics for a Diverse Society* (Frankfort-Nachmias & Leon-Guerrero, 2009) or Chapter 13 of *Adventures in Social Research* (Babbie, Halley, Wagner, & Zaino, 2010).

Lambda (λ)

Lambda is a measure of association for nominal variables. It ranges from 0 to 1. When lambda equals 0, then there is no association; none of the variation in the dependent variable can be explained by the variation in the independent variable. When lambda equals 1, then it is a perfect (deterministic) association; 100% (all) of the variation in the dependent variable can be explained by the variation of the independent variable.

To compute lambda by hand, we would calculate E1 and E2. E1 gives the number of errors that would be made predicting the dependent variable while ignoring the information available in the independent variable. E2 represents the errors of prediction of the dependent variable taking into account the information obtained from the independent variable. Using those errors, lambda is calculated as follows:

$$\lambda = \frac{E1 - E2}{E1}$$

Before computing lambda, turn off the split file feature if you haven't already done so or restarted SPSS/PASW Statistics. Open the "Split File" dialog box as follows:

DATA → SPLIT FILE . . .

Now, choose "Analyze all cases, do not create groups" and click "OK." SPSS/PASW Statistics will now not split the file, so that all cases in the dataset will be analyzed.

To compute lambda for the relationship between race and view on capital punishment, begin again by selecting the cross-tabulation menu:

ANALYZE → DESCRIPTIVE STATISTICS → CROSSTABS . . .

Now, when presented the "Crosstabs" dialog box, and after entering the variables of interest ("race" and "cappun" in this case), select the "Statistics" button. You will be given the following dialog box:

Under the "Nominal" heading, select "Lambda." This will instruct SPSS/PASW Statistics to add lambda to the things it will present in the output. Now, click "Continue" in the "Statistics" dialog box, and then "OK" in the prior dialog box. Below is an image from the output SPSS/PASW will produce:

Directional Measures

			Value	Asymp. Std. Error[a]	Approx. T[b]	Approx. Sig.
Nominal by Nominal	Lambda	Symmetric	.023	.013	1.772	.076
		cappun FAVOR OR OPPOSE DEATH PENALTY FOR MURDER Dependent	.044	.024	1.772	.076
		race RACE OF RESPONDENT Dependent	.000	.000	[c]	[c]
	Goodman and Kruskal tau	cappun FAVOR OR OPPOSE DEATH PENALTY FOR MURDER Dependent	.050	.010		.000[d]
		race RACE OF RESPONDENT Dependent	.029	.006		.000[d]

a. Not assuming the null hypothesis.

b. Using the asymptotic standard error assuming the null hypothesis.

c. Cannot be computed because the asymptotic standard error equals zero.

d. Based on chi-square approximation

Typically, lambda is presented as an asymmetrical measure of association; this is the case in *Social Statistics for a Diverse Society* (Frankfort-Nachmias & Leon-Guerrero, 2006) as well as in *Adventures in Social Research* (Babbie et al., 2010). Given that, the value of lambda to be used can be found in the "Value" column in the row indicating the correct dependent variable. In this case, "cappun" (favor or oppose death penalty for murder) is the appropriate dependent variable. We see that lambda is 0.044, but that it is *not* statistically significant ($p = 0.076$). The p refers to the probability that the result is due to chance; a smaller number ($p = 0.05$ or less) would indicate statistical significance.

Gamma (γ), Kendall's Tau-*b*, and Somers' *d*

*Gamma, Kendall's tau-*b, and *Somers'* d are all measures of association for ordinal and dichotomous nominal variables. All three of these PRE statistics can take on values ranging from −1 to +1. A value of +1 indicates that there is a deterministic and positive association, such that all of the variation in the dependent variable is accounted for by the variation in the independent variable. A value of −1 indicates, again, that there is a deterministic association, but that it is negative. While all of the variation in the dependent variable is accounted for by the variation in the independent variable, the association is in the opposite (negative) direction. When gamma, Kendall's tau-*b*, or Somers' *d* is equal to 0, this is an indication that there is no association; none of the variation in the dependent variable can be explained by the variation in the independent variable. Of course, the closer the value of either of these measures is to zero, the weaker the association. The closer the value is to either +1 or −1, the stronger the association, in the respective direction.

Each of these three measures is calculated using the concept of pairs. If all possible dyads were selected from a dataset, and we looked at how each value in the pair "scored" on each of two variables, we could see whether they both score higher on one than the other or whether one scores higher on one variable and lower on the other. In the former case, the pairs are called *same order pairs* and denoted *Ns*, while pairs in the latter case are labeled *inverse ordered pairs* and denoted *Nd*. We could also see if the two values in each pair have the same score on one or both variables (independent variable X or dependent variable Y). Those with equal values (tied) on the independent variables are represented by *Tx*, while those tied on the dependent variable are marked with *Ty*.

Gamma (γ), sometimes referred to as Goodman and Kruskal's gamma, is a symmetrical measure of association that is calculated as follows:

$$\gamma = \frac{Ns - Nd}{N + Nd}$$

Kendall's tau-*b* is also a symmetrical measure of association. The following equation shows how Kendall's tau-*b* is calculated using pairs:

$$tau\text{-}b = \frac{Ns - Nd}{\sqrt{(Ns + Nd + Tx)(Ns + Nd + Ty)}}$$

Somers' *d* is an asymmetrical measure of association; SPSS/PASW Statistics uses the term "directional measure" to describe asymmetrical measures. Somers' *d* is calculated as follows:

$$d = \frac{Ns - Nd}{Ns + Nd + Ty}$$

To compute measures of association like gamma, Kendall's tau-b, or Somers' d, use the following guidelines:

ANALYZE → DESCRIPTIVE STATISTICS → CROSSTABS . . .

You will be given a "Crosstabs" dialog box. For this example, select "satfin" as the row variable, and "satjob" as the column variable. "Satfin" is the variable representing how satisfied the respondent was with his or her financial situation. "Satjob" reveals the level of satisfaction that the respondent feels about his or her job or housework.

Now, click the "Cells" button. The following dialog box will appear:

In the "Cell Display" dialog box, make sure that "Observed" counts are selected and that "Column" percentages have been requested. Now, click "Continue." You will be returned to the "Crosstabs" dialog box. Here, click the "Statistics" button. You will be given the following dialog box:

In this box, select gamma, Somers' *d*, and Kendall's tau-*b*. Click "Continue," and then click "OK" once you are returned to the original "Crosstabs" dialog box. The tables below come from the output that SPSS/PASW Statistics will create.

satfin SATISFACTION WITH FINANCIAL SITUATION * satjob JOB OR HOUSEWORK Crosstabulation

			satjob JOB OR HOUSEWORK				
			1 VERY SATISFIED	2 MOD. SATISFIED	3 A LITTLE DISSAT	4 VERY DISSATISFIED	Total
satfin SATISFACTION WITH FINANCIAL SITUATION	1 SATISFIED	Count	274	94	18	3	389
		% within satjob JOB OR HOUSEWORK	35.4%	16.5%	13.4%	5.7%	25.4%
	2 MORE OR LESS	Count	331	262	50	14	657
		% within satjob JOB OR HOUSEWORK	42.7%	46.0%	37.3%	26.4%	42.9%
	3 NOT AT ALL SAT	Count	170	214	66	36	486
		% within satjob JOB OR HOUSEWORK	21.9%	37.5%	49.3%	67.9%	31.7%
Total		Count	775	570	134	53	1532
		% within satjob JOB OR HOUSEWORK	100.0%	100.0%	100.0%	100.0%	100.0%

Note that the standard cross-tabulation is produced above and gives an overview by column percents of the relationship between the two variables.

Directional Measures

			Value	Asymp. Std. Error[a]	Approx. T[b]	Approx. Sig.
Ordinal by Ordinal	Somers' d	Symmetric	.256	.022	11.608	.000
		satfin SATISFACTION WITH FINANCIAL SITUATION Dependent	.268	.023	11.608	.000
		satjob JOB OR HOUSEWORK Dependent	.245	.021	11.608	.000

a. Not assuming the null hypothesis.

b. Using the asymptotic standard error assuming the null hypothesis.

The value for Somers' d is located in the "Value" column in the row with the appropriate variable listed as the dependent variable. (Note that since Somers' d is asymmetrical, the two values given, where the dependent variables are different, turn out to be different.) Somers' d is statistically significant in this case ($p = 0.000$) regardless of which variable is treated as the dependent variable. Its value is 0.268 with "satfin" treated as the dependent variable. We would interpret this by saying that 26.8% of the variation in satisfaction with financial situation can be accounted for by the variation in satisfaction with job or housework. Somers' d would be 0.245 with "satjob" as the dependent variable. This tells us that 24.5% of the variation in job satisfaction can be explained by the variation in satisfaction with financial situation. Either way you look at it, errors of prediction are reduced by about one quarter.

Symmetric Measures

		Value	Asymp. Std. Error[a]	Approx. T[b]	Approx. Sig.
Ordinal by Ordinal	Kendall's tau-b	.256	.022	11.608	.000
	Gamma	.405	.033	11.608	.000
N of Valid Cases		1532			

a. Not assuming the null hypothesis.

b. Using the asymptotic standard error assuming the null hypothesis.

Above, Kendall's tau-b is given as 0.256. It is also statistically significant, where $p = 0.000$. When Kendall's tau-$b = 0.256$, we can say that 25.6% of the variation in the dependent variable can be accounted for by the variation in the independent variable.

Note the value for gamma: 0.405. It, too, is statistically significant ($p = 0.000$). When $\gamma = 0.405$, we can say that 40.5% of the variation in the dependent variable can be explained by the variation in the independent variable.

References

Babbie, E., Halley, F., Wagner, W. E., III, & Zaino, J. (2010). *Adventures in social research: Data analysis using IBM® SPSS® Statistics* (7th ed.). Thousand Oaks, CA: Pine Forge Press.

Frankfort-Nachmias, C., & Leon-Guerrero, A. (2006). *Social statistics for a diverse society* (4th ed.). Thousand Oaks, CA: Pine Forge Press.

Frankfort-Nachmias, C., & Leon-Guerrero, A. (2009). *Social statistics for a diverse society* (5th ed.). Thousand Oaks, CA: Pine Forge Press.

7

Correlation and Regression Analysis

Regression analysis allows us to predict one variable from information that we have about other variables. In this chapter, linear regression will be discussed. Linear regression is a type of analysis that is performed on interval and ratio variables (labeled "scale" variables in SPSS/PASW Statistics. Though, through the use of dummy variables, for instance, it is possible to incorporate data from variables with lower levels of measurement (i.e., nominal and ordinal variables). We will begin with a bivariate regression example and then add some more detail to the analysis.

Bivariate Regression

In the case of bivariate regression, researchers are interested in predicting the value of the dependent variable, Y, from the information they have about the independent variable, X. We will use the example below, where respondent's occupational prestige score is predicted from number of years of education. Choose the following menus to begin the bivariate regression analysis:

ANALYZE → REGRESSION → LINEAR . . .

The "Linear Regression" dialog box will appear. Initially, select the variables of interest and drag them into the appropriate areas for dependent and independent variables. The variable "prestg80," respondent's occupational prestige score, should be moved to the "Dependent" area, and "educ," respondent's number of years of education, should be moved to the "Independent" area. Now, simply click "OK." The following SPSS/PASW Statistics output will be produced.

Model Summary

Model	R	R Square	Adjusted R Square	Std. Error of the Estimate
1	.526[a]	.277	.276	11.810

a. Predictors: (Constant), educ HIGHEST YEAR OF SCHOOL COMPLETED

In the first column of the Model Summary, the output will yield Pearson's r (in the column labeled "R"), followed in the next column by r-square (r^2). SPSS/PASW Statistics also computes an adjusted r^2 for those interested in using that value. R-square, like lambda, gamma, and Somers' d, is a PRE (proportional reduction in error) statistic that reveals the proportional reduction in error by introducing the dependent variable(s). In this case, $r^2 = 0.277$, which means 27.7% of the variation in occupational prestige score is explained by the variation in years of education.

ANOVA[b]

Model		Sum of Squares	df	Mean Square	F	Sig.
1	Regression	102063.694	1	102063.694	731.743	.000[a]
	Residual	266965.009	1914	139.480		
	Total	369028.703	1915			

a. Predictors: (Constant), educ HIGHEST YEAR OF SCHOOL COMPLETED

b. Dependent Variable: prestg80 RS OCCUPATIONAL PRESTIGE SCORE (1980)

ANOVA (analysis of variance) values, including the F statistic, are given in the above table of the linear regression output.

Coefficients[a]

Model		Unstandardized Coefficients		Standardized Coefficients		
		B	Std. Error	Beta	t	Sig.
1	(Constant)	11.542	1.223		9.438	.000
	educ HIGHEST YEAR OF SCHOOL COMPLETED	2.394	.089	.526	27.051	.000

a. Dependent Variable: prestg80 RS OCCUPATIONAL PRESTIGE SCORE (1980)

The coefficients table reveals the actual regression coefficients for the regression equation, as well as their statistical significance. In the "Unstandardized Coefficients" column, and in the "B" subcolumn, the coefficients are given. In this case the "b" value for number of years of education completed is 2.394. The "a" value, or constant, is 11.542. By looking in the last column (Sig.), you can see that both values are statistically significant ($p = 0.000$). Remember, the p refers to the probability that the result is due to chance, so smaller numbers are better. The standard in social sciences is usually 0.05; something is statistically significant if the p value is less than 0.05. We would write the regression equation describing the model computed by SPSS/PASW Statistics as follows:

$$\hat{Y} = bX + a \rightarrow \hat{Y} = 2.394X^* + 11.542^*$$

*Statistically significant at the $p \leq 0.05$ level

The coefficient in the bivariate regression model above can be interpreted to mean that each additional year of education provides a 2.394-point predicted increase in occupational prestige score. The constant gives the predicted occupational prestige score when years of education is zero; however, as is often the case with a regression equation, that may be beyond the range of the data for reasonable prediction. In other words, if no one had zero or near zero years of education in the sample, then range of the data upon which the prediction was calculated did not include such, and we should be cautious in making predictions at those levels.

Correlation

Information about correlation tells us the extent to which variables are related. Below, the Pearson method of computing correlation is requested through SPSS/PASW Statistics. To examine a basic correlation between two variables, use the following menus:

ANALYZE → CORRELATE → BIVARIATE . . .

In the "Bivariate Correlations" dialog box, choose the variables that you wish to examine. In the above case, "male" (a dummy variable representing sex, described in further detail below, under "Multiple Regression") and "educ," representing years of education, have been selected. For now, "male" is a recoded version of the sex variable, where a male is coded as 1 and a female is coded as 0. Thus, a "1" indicates "male" and a "0" indicates "not male," with a proportional range in between. This allows us to treat a nominal dichotomy as an interval/ratio variable and then use it in regression and correlation analysis. The output that results is shown in the following table.

Correlations

		educ HIGHEST YEAR OF SCHOOL COMPLETED	male Male Dummy Variable
educ HIGHEST YEAR OF SCHOOL COMPLETED	Pearson Correlation	1	.006
	Sig. (2-tailed)		.772
	N	2018	2018
male Male Dummy Variable	Pearson Correlation	.006	1
	Sig. (2-tailed)	.772	
	N	2018	2023

Note that in the output, the correlation is an extremely low 0.006, which is not statistically significant ($p = 0.772$). This tells us that being male is not correlated with higher years of education.

It is also possible to produce partial correlations. Suppose you are interested in examining the correlation between occupational prestige and education. Further suppose you wish to determine the way that sex impacts that correlation. Follow the following menus to produce a partial correlation:

ANALYZE → CORRELATE → PARTIAL . . .

In the "Partial Correlations" dialog box, you will be able to select the variables among which you wish to examine a correlation. You will also be able to select the control variable, around which partial correlations will be computed. In this case, years of education ("educ") and occupational prestige score ("prestg80") have been selected for correlation analysis. The control variable is "male." (It is also possible to include more than one control variable.)

SPSS/PASW Statistics provides the following output.

Correlations

Control Variables			educ HIGHEST YEAR OF SCHOOL COMPLETED	prestg80 RS OCCUPATIO NAL PRESTIGE SCORE (1980)
male Male Dummy Variable	educ HIGHEST YEAR OF SCHOOL COMPLETED	Correlation	1.000	.526
		Significance (2-tailed)	.	.000
		df	0	1913
	prestg80 RS OCCUPATIONAL PRESTIGE SCORE (1980)	Correlation	.526	1.000
		Significance (2-tailed)	.000	.
		df	1913	0

Here, the correlation is noteworthy, at 0.526, and is statistically significant ($p = 0.000$). Correlation information about variables is useful to have before constructing regression models. Should you want to know more, many textbooks in statistics and research methods have detailed discussions about how this information aids in regression analysis.

Multiple Regression

Now, suppose a researcher wished to include one or more additional independent variables in the bivariate regression analysis. This is very easy to do using SPSS/PASW Statistics. All you need do is move the additional variables into the "Independent(s)" area in the "Linear Regression" dialog box, as seen below:

ANALYZE → REGRESSION → LINEAR . . .

Since linear regression requires interval-ratio variables, one must take care when incorporating variables, such as sex, race/ethnicity, religion, and the like. By creating dummy variables from the categories of these nominal variables, you can add this information to the regression equation.

To do this, use the recode function (for more information about recoding variables, see Chapter 2: Transforming Variables). Create a dichotomous variable for all but one category, the "omitted" comparison category/attribute, and insert each of those dichotomies into the "Independent(s)" area. The number of dummy variables necessary for a given variable will be equal to $K–1$, where K is the number of categories of the variable. Dichotomies are an exception to the cumulative property of levels of measurement, which tells us that variables measured at higher levels can be treated at lower levels, but *not* vice versa. Dichotomies can be coded to be treated as if they are at any level of measurement.

For the case of sex, we already have a dichotomy exclusive of transgender and other conditions, so the recode just changes this to one variable: "male." (Alternatively, you could have changed it to "female.") The coding should be binary: 1 for affirmation of the attribute, 0 for respondents not possessing the attribute. Now, as was entered into the previous dialog box, just select the new recoded variable, "male," from the variable bank on the left, and drag it into the "Independent(s)" area on the right. You may need to set the variable property to scale in the Variable View tab of the Data Editor window, so that SPSS/PASW Statistics will allow that variable to be included in the regression analysis. Newer versions of SPSS/PASW Statistics track variable types and often will not allow you to include variables with lower levels of measurement in analyses requiring variables with higher levels of measurement.

After recoding as necessary and dragging your variables of interest into their respective areas, click the "Plots" button, and you will be given the "Plots" dialog box:

Here, you can avail yourself of a couple of useful graphics: a histogram and a normal probability plot. Click each box to request them. Then click "Continue."

When you are returned to the "Linear Regression" dialog box, now select the "Statistics" button. The following dialog box will appear:

There are a number of options, including descriptive statistics, which you may select to be included in the SPSS/PASW Statistics linear regression output. For now, leave the defaults checked as shown, and click "Continue" in this box; then click "OK" when returned to the "Linear Regression" dialog box.

Below, find tables from the SPSS/PASW Statistics output that results. The first two tables give the same sort of information as before in the bivariate regression case: Pearson's r (correlation coefficient), r^2 (PRE), and ANOVA (analysis of variance) values.

Model Summary[b]

Model	R	R Square	Adjusted R Square	Std. Error of the Estimate
1	.526[a]	.277	.276	11.813

a. Predictors: (Constant), male Male Dummy Variable, educ HIGHEST YEAR OF SCHOOL COMPLETED

b. Dependent Variable: prestg80 RS OCCUPATIONAL PRESTIGE SCORE (1980)

In this case $r^2 = 0.277$, which means 27.7% of the variation in occupational prestige score ("prestg80") is explained by the variation in the independent variables: years of education ("educ") and sex ("male").

ANOVA[b]

Model		Sum of Squares	df	Mean Square	F	Sig.
1	Regression	102078.689	2	51039.345	365.755	.000[a]
	Residual	266950.014	1913	139.545		
	Total	369028.703	1915			

a. Predictors: (Constant), male Male Dummy Variable, educ HIGHEST YEAR OF SCHOOL COMPLETED

b. Dependent Variable: prestg80 RS OCCUPATIONAL PRESTIGE SCORE (1980)

The "Coefficients" table (below), again, provides the information that can be used to construct the regression model/equation. Note that the dummy variable, "male," was not statistically significant.

$$\hat{Y} = bX_1 + bX_2 + a \rightarrow \hat{Y} = 2.394X_1^* - 0.177X_2 + 11.629^*$$

*Statistically significant at the $p \leq 0.05$ level

The X_1 coefficient ("educ," years of education) can be interpreted to mean that each additional year of education provides a 2.394-point predicted increase in occupational prestige score. The X_2 coefficient ("male," dummy variable for sex) can be interpreted to mean that males have an occupational prestige score 0.177 points less than non-males (females). However, pay attention to the statistical significances. While the constant and years of education are both statistically significant with $p = 0.000$, the "male" variable has a p value of 0.743, and so sex is not statistically significant in this equation.

Coefficients[a]

Model		Unstandardized Coefficients		Standardized Coefficients	t	Sig.
		B	Std. Error	Beta		
1	(Constant)	11.629	1.252		9.288	.000
	educ HIGHEST YEAR OF SCHOOL COMPLETED	2.394	.089	.526	27.038	.000
	male Male Dummy Variable	-.177	.541	-.006	-.328	.743

a. Dependent Variable: prestg80 RS OCCUPATIONAL PRESTIGE SCORE (1980)

The two graphics that follow show a histogram of the regression standardized residual for the dependent variable as well as the observed by expected cumulative probability for the dependent variable, occupational prestige.

It is possible to add additional variables to your linear regression model, such as those in the dialog box featured below. Interval-ratio variables may be included, as well as dummy variables, along with others such as interaction variables. Interaction variables may be computed using the compute function (in the "Transform" menu). More information about computing variables can be found in Chapter 2: Transforming Variables. The computation would consist of variable1*variable2 = interaction variable.

8

Logistic Regression Analysis

M uch like ordinary least squares (OLS) linear regression analysis (see Chapter 7: Correlation and Regression Analysis), logistic regression analysis allows us to predict values on a dependent variable from information that we have about other (independent) variables. Logistic regression analysis is also known as *logit* regression analysis, and it is performed on a dichotomous dependent variable and dichotomous independent variables. Through the use of dummy variables, it is possible to incorporate independent variables that have more than two categories. The dependent variable usually measures the presence of something or the likelihood that a future event will happen; examples include predictions of whether students will graduate on time or whether a student will graduate at all.

Preparing Variables for Use in Logistic Regression Analysis

In order to be able to compute a logistic regression model with SPSS/PASW Statistics, all of the variables to be used should be dichotomous. Furthermore, they should be coded as "1" representing existence of an attribute, and "0" to denote none of that attribute. This may involve considerable recoding, even from dichotomies between "1" and "2" to dichotomies between "0" and "1."

For our example logistic regression, suppose we were interested in work status as predicted by gender and race/ethnicity. In Chapter 7: Correlation and Regression Analysis, "male," a dummy variable for sex, was created; the "1–2" dichotomy was transformed into a "0–1" dichotomy, where 0 = female and 1 = male.

The GSS variable "wrkstat" has eight categories, so we will need to decide what one category we want to examine. In recoding this variable, we create a variable that shows whether the respondent is (a) working full-time, or (b) not working full-time. To carry out this transformation, follow the instructions below:

TRANSFORM → RECODE INTO DIFFERENT VARIABLES . . .

In the dialog box that appears, find the original variable, "wrkstat," and drag it into the "Numeric Variable → Output Variable" area. Now, choose a new name (the example here is "wrkstatD") and label (Employed Full-time(D)). Click the "Change" button, and verify that the new variable name change has been marked next to the original variable name. Now click the "Old and New Values . . ." button.

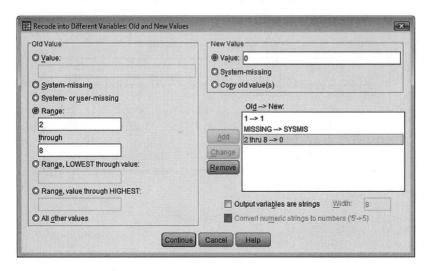

In the "Old and New Values" dialog box, have the old value of 1 (employed full-time) coded as 1 in the new variable. All other values, or those from 2 to 8, should be coded as 0, since they represent individuals who are not employed full-time. Be sure to include an instruction to SPSS/PASW Statistics for missing cases, like the one in the screen image above.

Now, click "Continue" and then "OK" in the "Recode into Different Variables" box, and the new variable will be created. You will want to update information about "wrkstatD" in the Variable View tab of the Data Editor window, such as its measure (nominal), decimals (0), and so forth, as shown below:

You can verify the new variable in the Data View window. You could also produce a frequency distribution of the new variable, "wrkstatD," to verify the transformation and observe the distribution, as given below:

wrkstatD Employed Full-time (D)

		Frequency	Percent	Valid Percent	Cumulative Percent
Valid	0	1018	50.3	50.4	50.4
	1	1003	49.6	49.6	100.0
	Total	2021	99.9	100.0	
Missing	System	2	.1		
Total		2023	100.0		

Notice the approximately even distribution of "wrkstatD" (full-time employment dichotomy). If there were only a small percentage in either category, the variable would not be suitable for use in this analysis and would need to be recoded in some other way to capture more variation.

Creating a Set of Dummy Variables to Represent a Multicategory Nominal Variable

Our other independent variables will represent race/ethnicity. We will use the four-category race variable that was recoded using the original race variable and the variable "Hispanic." The categories are: White, Black, Other, and Hispanic. Since there are four categories, we will need to create three dummy variables. The number of dummy variables in a set that represents a nominal variable is equal to $K-1$, where K is the number of categories. To do this, first produce a frequency distribution, as follows:

ANALYZE → DESCRIPTIVE STATISTICS → FREQUENCIES . . .

After requesting the frequency for race (as recoded with additional information from the variable "Hispanic," in Chapter 2: Transforming Variables), we get the following chart:

race RACE OF RESPONDENT

		Frequency	Percent	Valid Percent	Cumulative Percent
Valid	1 WHITE	1429	70.6	70.6	70.6
	2 BLACK	272	13.4	13.4	84.1
	3 OTHER	85	4.2	4.2	88.3
	4 HISPANIC	237	11.7	11.7	100.0
	Total	2023	100.0	100.0	

Since the "Other" category is relatively small at just 4.2% of valid cases, you might wish to define those in that category as missing and proceed with a three-category variable (White, Black, and Hispanic), producing two dummy variables: $K-1 = 2$.

We will proceed with all four categories. Let's make four dummy variables, and then we'll choose which three to use for the analysis, based on which groups we wish to compare. First select the following menus:

TRANSFORM → COMPUTE VARIABLE . . .

Name the target variable; in this case it will be "White." Now, set all cases in the new variable equal to zero, as above. Then, click "OK." You can verify in the Data Editor window that a new variable has been appended to the data file that has all zeros as data.

Next, we will want to correct those cases for which the respondent was white. To do that, again select these menus:

TRANSFORM → COMPUTE VARIABLE . . .

Now, change the value in the Numeric Expression area to 1. Then, click "If . . ." in the lower left corner of the "Compute Variable" box. The following dialog box will appear:

Select the radio button next to "Include if case satisfies condition:". Then type "race=1" in the box beneath. Now click "Continue" and then "OK." You'll be given the following warning. Be sure to click "OK" to verify that you do wish to alter some of the data in this variable.

Now, let's use the same procedure to create the variable "Black." Click the following menus:

TRANSFORM → COMPUTE VARIABLE . . .

First, click the "Reset" button to eliminate information from the prior transformation. Then set all of the cases in the new variable, "Black," equal to zero. Then click "OK." Once you verify the creation of the new variable in your Data Editor window, again click these menus:

TRANSFORM → COMPUTE VARIABLE . . .

Here, in the Numeric Expression area, you will enter 1. Now, click the "If . . ." button, and in the dialog box that appears, choose the "Include if case satisfies condition:" radio button and enter the equation "race=2" in the box beneath. Now, click "Continue" and then "OK."

Next, follow the same procedure for "Other/Others" and "Hispanic/Latino," as described below:

1. For "Others," select TRANSFORM → COMPUTE VARIABLE . . . , and then set Others = 0. Next, using the Compute command, set Others = 1, IF: race = 3. (We are using the name "Others" instead of "Other," since "Other" represents another variable in the GSS original data file. You are free to label this new variable as "Other," though that would delete the original variable that contains data about other Protestant denominations.)

2. For "Latino," select TRANSFORM → COMPUTE VARIABLE . . . , then set Latino = 0. Next, using the Compute command, set Latino = 1, IF: race = 4. (We are using the name "Latino," since "Hispanic" represents another variable in the GSS original data file. In fact, the original variable, "Hispanic," contains information that we used to recode the very race variable we are using here by adding a fourth category in Chapter 2: Transforming Variables. You could rename "Hispanic" to something else and use that name here if you wish.)

Now, for all four new variables, go to the Variable View window and edit the settings to reflect each new variable's decimals (0), measure (nominal), and so on.

The method we have used above creates dummy variables in two steps: (1) Name the new variable and set all cases equal to zero, and (2) change the settings for the appropriate cases corresponding to the race/ethnicity equal to one. Note that we are able to set the variables equal to zero first, without worrying about missing cases only because there happen to be no missing cases for the race variable. If there were missing cases, we would need to handle those cases with the Compute command, as well.

Logistic Regression Analysis

Choose the following menus to begin the logistic regression analysis:

ANALYZE → REGRESSION → BINARY LOGISTIC . . .

Select "wrkstatD" as the dependent variable by dragging it from the column on the left into the box under "Dependent." Independent variables will go in the box labeled "Covariates." For gender, use "male." For race/ethnicity, think about which category you want to use as a reference. Whatever results you get will reveal whether other groups are more or less likely to have full-time employment than the reference (left out) category.

In this case, if we omit "White," then the comparison can be made from other groups to whites. Let's use that in our example. Enter the three other dummy variables as they appear in the screen image above. Then click "OK." A selection from the output produced is as follows. See "Interpreting Odds Ratios" at the end of this chapter for an explanation of how to interpret the central parts of the logistic regression output.

Model Summary

Step	-2 Log likelihood	Cox & Snell R Square	Nagelkerke R Square
1	2709.909ᵃ	.044	.059

a. Estimation terminated at iteration number 3 because parameter estimates changed by less than .001.

Variables in the Equation

		B	S.E.	Wald	df	Sig.	Exp(B)
Step 1[a]	male	.836	.091	83.588	1	.000	2.308
	Black	.127	.135	.885	1	.347	1.136
	Latino	.330	.144	5.214	1	.022	1.391
	Others	.150	.229	.431	1	.511	1.162
	Constant	-.460	.069	44.849	1	.000	.631

a. Variable(s) entered on step 1: male, Black, Latino, Others.

Logistic Regression Using a Categorical Covariate Without Dummy Variables

The logistic regression command has a built-in way to analyze a nominal/categorical variable like our recoded race variable. The results produced will be identical to those described earlier in this chapter, and there is no need to create dummy variables. There are, however, some situations in SPSS/PASW Statistics where you must create and use dummy variables, and that method directly exposes the user to how the data are being treated and analyzed. The following method should be used only by those who fully understand the nature of categorical analysis within a logistic regression model, and it should be noted that there are limitations: The reference category can be only the *first* or *last* category of the variable to be used as a covariate. In the case of the race variable, "White" is the first category and "Latino" is the last category. Had we wished to use "Black" or "Others" as a reference category, we would need either to have created dummy variables as above or to have recoded "race" to suit our needs. Another limitation will be addressed toward the end of this chapter; it concerns complications when using certain methods of inclusion for variables.

In any case, follow the instructions below to produce the logistic regression equation using the categorical variable method:

ANALYZE → REGRESSION → BINARY LOGISTIC . . .

As before, select "wrkstatD" as the dependent variable. Also, add "male" as one of the covariates. Now, simply add "race" as one of the covariates. You cannot stop here and run the analysis; the results would be without useful interpretation. So it is necessary to tell SPSS/PASW Statistics that "race" is a categorical/nominal variable and to tell it which category should be the designated reference category (and therefore "left out" of the analysis in the same way it was in our utilization of dummy variables). To do this, click the "Categorical" button . . .

Now, in the dialog box with which you are presented, select "race" from the list of covariates on the left, and drag it into the box under "Categorical Covariates." Then select "First" as the reference category, and click the "Change" button. You should notice the word "first" appear as in the screen image above. Now click "Continue" and then "OK." The output from this command is displayed and interpreted in the following section.

Interpreting Odds Ratios

Logistic regression uses natural logarithms to produce a logistic curve as a predictor, whereas you may remember that OLS linear regression uses the least squares method to produce a straight line as a predictor. The coefficients in a logistic regression model can be exponentiated as log odds ratios. Selected output from the logistic regression command, above, has been printed below:

Model Summary

Step	-2 Log likelihood	Cox & Snell R Square	Nagelkerke R Square
1	2709.909[a]	.044	.059

a. Estimation terminated at iteration number 3 because parameter estimates changed by less than .001.

Variables in the Equation

	B	S.E.	Wald	df	Sig.	Exp(B)
Step 1[a] male	.836	.091	83.588	1	.000	2.308
race			5.746	3	.125	
race(1)	.127	.135	.885	1	.347	1.136
race(2)	.150	.229	.431	1	.511	1.162
race(3)	.330	.144	5.214	1	.022	1.391
Constant	-.460	.069	44.849	1	.000	.631

a. Variable(s) entered on step 1: male, race.

Notice that in the Model Summary box, two different r-squares (r^2) are presented: Cox and Snell as well as Nagelkerke. While computed differently, these numbers can be interpreted in much the same way as r^2 itself, the coefficient of determination. (See Chapter 7: Correlation and Regression Analysis, for more details on PRE [proportional reduction in error] statistics and the coefficient of determination.)

In the "Variables in the Equation" box, the coefficients themselves are found in column "B," but they have been exponentiated in the column "Exp(B)." This value tells how much more or less likely a subject in the designated category is to be in the affirmative category on the dependent variable (employed full-time) than a subject in the omitted reference category. For the coefficient, male, the odds ratio is 2.308, and it is statistically significant ($p = 0.000$ in the "Sig." column); therefore, men are 2.308 times more likely than women to be employed full-time and not fall into some other category of employment.

The first race row in the "Variables in the Equation" box is the omitted reference category, White. Notice that there is no coefficient or exponentiated coefficient in that row. In the rows below, "race(1)" represents the next category, Black; "race(2)" represents the third category, Other/Others; and "race(3)" represents the last category, Hispanic/Latino. The only category (or dummy variable) that is statistically significant for race is Hispanic/Latino ($p = 0.022$). The exponentiated coefficient reveals that Hispanics were 1.391 times more likely than those in the reference category (Whites) to have full-time employment and not fall in some other category of the original variable: employed part-time, retired, keeping house, and so forth. Comparisons can directly be made only with the reference category.

To have SPSS/PASW Statistics help produce the equation with the best set of statistically significant variables, so that you will not need to try each combination manually, you can select a different option from the pull down menu in the "Method" pane in the "Logistic Regression" dialog box, such as "Backward: Conditional," as demonstrated below. While this method works effectively when using the dummy variable approach to logistic regression analysis, it is not effective with the categorical variable method.

From the output produced, the following selection reveals the final coefficients. Notice that each step removes variables that are not statistically significant and that contribute the least to the model. In the third step, the final model is provided. The number of steps that are required by SPSS/PASW Statistics to produce the final equation depends on numerous factors.

Notice that in our simple example, the final equation is very similar to the model we produced above, though the nonsignificant dummy variables have been removed from the model. Notice, too, that the value of r^2 (both Cox & Snell, and Nagelkerke) is not reduced as a result of the removal of variables (i.e., in conjunction with the other variables in the equation, the variation in the deleted variables did not account for any variation in the dependent variable). Granted, the Nagelkerke calculation did decline slightly from 0.059 to 0.058.

Model Summary

Step	-2 Log likelihood	Cox & Snell R Square	Nagelkerke R Square
1	2709.909[a]	.044	.059
2	2710.341[a]	.044	.059
3	2711.120[a]	.044	.058

a. Estimation terminated at iteration number 3 because parameter estimates changed by less than .001.

Variables in the Equation

		B	S.E.	Wald	df	Sig.	Exp(B)
Step 1[a]	male	.836	.091	83.588	1	.000	2.308
	Black	.127	.135	.885	1	.347	1.136
	Others	.150	.229	.431	1	.511	1.162
	Latino	.330	.144	5.214	1	.022	1.391
	Constant	-.460	.069	44.849	1	.000	.631
Step 2[a]	male	.837	.091	83.877	1	.000	2.310
	Black	.119	.135	.779	1	.377	1.126
	Latino	.321	.144	4.990	1	.025	1.379
	Constant	-.453	.068	44.723	1	.000	.636
Step 3[a]	male	.835	.091	83.487	1	.000	2.304
	Latino	.303	.142	4.536	1	.033	1.354
	Constant	-.433	.064	45.904	1	.000	.648

a. Variable(s) entered on step 1: male, Black, Others, Latino.

9

Testing Hypotheses
Using Means and
Cross-Tabulation

S PSS/PASW Statistics allows for automatic testing of hypotheses without having to make a computation and check a cut point in a table in the back of a statistics book. The actual statistical significance is presented with the results.

Comparing Means

This section explains how to examine differences between two means. Comparing means between groups requires having a variable that will allow for a division into the appropriate groups, in the same way that it is required to split a data file for a comparative analysis. (See Chapter 6: Cross-Tabulation and Measures of Association for Nominal and Ordinal Variables, for further details on using the Split File command.)

Suppose you are interested in comparing the occupational prestige scores of respondents and wish to examine the differences between men and women. Select the following menus:

ANALYZE → COMPARE MEANS → MEANS . . .

Additional layers can be requested by clicking "Next" and then adding the additional variable(s). The DATA → SPLIT FILE option can also be used to compare groups across categories/attributes of a variable. If you click on the "Options" button, the box shown below will appear, and you can customize the cell statistics that SPSS/PASW Statistics will report in the output.

Select those statistics that you wish to be reported, and drag them to the Cell Statistics area. After you click "Continue" and then "OK" in the "Means" dialog box, SPSS/PASW Statistics will generate the following output.

Report

prestg80 RS OCCUPATIONAL PRESTIGE SCORE (1980)

male Male Dum…	Mean	N	Std. Deviation
0 Female	43.92	1026	14.110
1 Male	43.61	895	13.634
Total	43.77	1921	13.887

A simple table is provided that displays mean, sample size, and standard deviation for the total sample, as well as for each category of the variable of interest: occupational prestige.

Comparing Means: Paired-Samples *t* Test

The paired-samples *t* test can be used when, for a given dataset, the means of all the values for each of two variables are to be compared. An example of such a dataset would be a data file containing scores for a group of people who have taken a particular pretest and then an identical posttest after some sort of stimulus had been administered. There are many situations where this method of analysis is appropriate.

From the 2008 GSS, we can look at parental education by parent's gender. In other words, we can compare the years of education completed by the respondents' fathers with those completed by the mothers. To begin, select the following menus:

ANALYZE → COMPARE MEANS → PAIRED SAMPLES T-TEST . . .

In order to move a complete entry into the Paired Variables area, you will need to select two variables from the variable bank on the left side of the dialog box. Once you have selected two variables and clicked the arrow for each (one right after the other), their names will appear under "Variable1" and "Variable2" for "Pair 1." Additional pairs may be added in subsequent rows.

Should you wish to change the confidence interval (note that the default is 95%), or change the way that missing cases are handled or excluded, click the "Options" button, and you will be given a dialog box to make those selections, as illustrated below.

Once you have made your selections, click "Continue" in the "Options" box, and then click "OK" in the "Paired-Samples T Test" box. What follows is output that SPSS/PASW Statistics will produce to fulfill your request:

Paired Samples Statistics

		Mean	N	Std. Deviation	Std. Error Mean
Pair 1	maeduc HIGHEST YEAR SCHOOL COMPLETED, MOTHER	11.52	1397	3.703	.099
	paeduc HIGHEST YEAR SCHOOL COMPLETED, FATHER	11.53	1397	4.199	.112

Paired Samples Correlations

		N	Correlation	Sig.
Pair 1	maeduc HIGHEST YEAR SCHOOL COMPLETED, MOTHER & paeduc HIGHEST YEAR SCHOOL COMPLETED, FATHER	1397	.679	.000

The two tables above give basic information, such as mean, sample size, standard deviation, standard error, and correlation between the two variables. Note that there is a statistically significant correlation between these two variables.

Paired Samples Test

		Paired Differences							
					95% Confidence Interval of the Difference				
		Mean	Std. Deviation	Std. Error Mean	Lower	Upper	t	df	Sig. (2-tailed)
Pair 1	maeduc HIGHEST YEAR SCHOOL COMPLETED, MOTHER - paeduc HIGHEST YEAR SCHOOL COMPLETED, FATHER	-.002	3.199	.086	-.170	.166	-.025	1396	.980

In the third table, results of the *t* test are displayed. Here, *t* = -0.025; it is not, however, statistically significant at the 0.05 level or better.

Comparing Means: Independent-Samples *t* Test

Independent-samples *t* tests allow us to compare the mean of a particular variable across independent groups. To look at an example using occupational prestige scale scores, use the following menu selections:

ANALYZE → COMPARE MEANS → INDEPENDENT-SAMPLES T TEST . . .

In this dialog box, drag the variable of interest, occupational prestige score ("prestg80"), into the Test Variable(s) area. Next, you will need to select the grouping variable. In the example above, "male" (dummy variable for gender) has been selected. Now, you need to inform SPSS/PASW Statistics which groups are to be compared. Click the "Define Groups" button.

In this "Define Groups" dialog box, fill in the category values for each group. Note that depending upon how the grouping variable is categorized, you have the option of selecting a cut point to define the groups. This could be done with age, test scores, and so on.

Click "Continue," which will take you back to the "Independent-Samples T Test" dialog box. You have the option of changing the confidence interval and method of case exclusion. To make those choices, click the "Options" button and you will be given the dialog box that follows:

Enter the changes you would like to make, if any, then click "Continue," and then click "OK" in the original dialog box. The output below will be generated by SPSS/PASW Statistics in response to your query:

Group Statistics

	male Male Dummy Variable	N	Mean	Std. Deviation	Std. Error Mean
prestg80 RS OCCUPATIONAL PRESTIGE SCORE (1980)	0 Female	1026	43.92	14.110	.440
	1 Male	895	43.61	13.634	.456

Independent Samples Test

		Levene's Test for Equality of Variances		t-test for Equality of Means					95% Confidence Interval of the Difference	
		F	Sig.	t	df	Sig. (2-tailed)	Mean Difference	Std. Error Difference	Lower	Upper
prestg80 RS OCCUPATIONAL PRESTIGE SCORE (1980)	Equal variances assumed	1.235	.266	.480	1919	.631	.305	.635	-.941	1.551
	Equal variances not assumed			.481	1899.039	.630	.305	.634	-.938	1.548

Basic statistics are given in the first table. The second table reveals the results and significance (or lack thereof in this case) of the *t* test. When the *t* test is statistically significant, we can say that the groups (males and females in this case) in the sample come from populations whose mean is different. Given the failure of the *t* test to achieve statistical significance in this case, we cannot make that claim.

Chi-Square (χ^2)

The *chi-square* test statistic is used to test statistical independence or goodness of fit. It is used for categorical data. Chi-square summarizes the differences between the observed frequencies (f_o) and the expected frequencies (f_e) in a bivariate table. The observed frequencies are those produced from the raw data. To compute the expected frequencies for any given cell in a bivariate table, multiply the column marginal (total) by the row marginal (total), and then divide by N (sample size). The obtained chi-square is then calculated as follows:

$$\chi^2 = \sum \frac{(f_o - f_e)}{f_e}.$$

There are two menu selections that will produce chi-square results: nonparametric tests and cross-tabulations. The former is demonstrated here, first using the legacy dialog (the way the function has been performed by prior versions of SPSS) and then using the new interface tools. To perform a chi-square analysis, choose the following menu options:

ANALYZE → NONPARAMETRIC TESTS → LEGACY DIALOGS → CHI-SQUARE . . .

Now, in the "Chi-square Test" dialog box, choose the variable that you would like to test. In this case, we chose "male," the dummy variable representing gender. For expected values, by leaving the button selected for "All categories equal," the expectation is that 50% of the respondents will be men and 50% will be women.

If you click on the "Options" button, you will be given a dialog box that allows you to request additional information and determine the method by which cases should be excluded.

When these decisions have been made, click "Continue," and then click "OK" in the "Chi-square Test" dialog box. The output that follows will be provided by SPSS/PASW Statistics:

male Male Dummy Variable

	Observed N	Expected N	Residual
0 Female	1094	1011.5	82.5
1 Male	929	1011.5	-82.5
Total	2023		

Test Statistics

	male Male Dummy Variable
Chi-square	13.458[a]
df	1
Asymp. Sig.	.000

a. 0 cells (.0%) have expected frequencies less than 5. The minimum expected cell frequency is 1011.5.

The first table provides the observed and expected amounts, and of course the residual or difference. The second table yields the chi-square value and degrees of freedom, and reveals whether the value is statistically significant. In this case, chi-square = 13.458 with 1 degree of freedom (df) and is statistically significant ($p = 0.000$).

The newer interface, among other things, offers greater assistance to the user in terms of selecting the appropriate statistic. It also provides a hypothesis-based response in the output, though it does not include the table of observed and expected values. Follow the menu options below to obtain chi-square results using this method:

ANALYZE → NONPARAMETRIC TESTS → ONE SAMPLE . . .

You will be presented with a dialog box like the one below. Choose the "Customize analysis" radio button, since you know that you want to calculate the chi-square statistic.

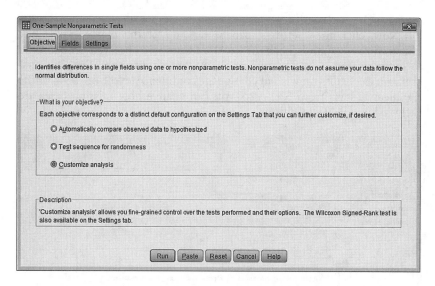

Now, click the "Fields" tab at the top of this dialog box. Here, make sure that "Customize field assignments" has been selected and choose the variable(s) that you want to test by including them in the Test Fields area. Below, "male" has been chosen.

Now, click the "Settings" tab at the top of the dialog box. Click "Customize tests" and check the box for "Compare observed probabilities to hypothesized (Chi-Square Test)." You can choose the "Test Options" entry on the left if you wish to change the confidence level from 95% or the significance level from 5%. Also, you can change how missing cases are excluded under "Test Options," as well.

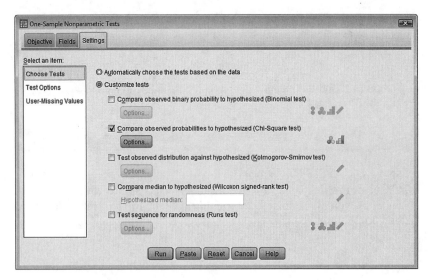

After you click "Run," SPSS/PASW Statistics will provide you with the following response.

Hypothesis Test Summary

	Null Hypothesis	Test	Sig.	Decision
1	The categories of Male Dummy Variable occur with equal probabilities.	One-Sample Chi-Square Test	.000	Reject the null hypothesis.

Asymptotic significances are displayed. The significance level is .05.

The output clearly indicates that the null hypothesis, that males and females occur in the population with equal probabilities, should be rejected. While there are more steps in this process than this example of the legacy dialog shows, the user has many more options and can request multiple statistical tests at once.

Chi-Square (χ^2) and Cross-Tabulation

If you would like to produce full cross-tabulations with chi-square test results, such as those detailed in Chapter 6: Cross-Tabulation and Measures of Association for Nominal and Ordinal Variables, see the following example by selecting the following menus:

ANALYZE → DESCRIPTIVE STATISTICS → CROSSTABS . . .

Click the "Statistics" button, and you will be presented with the following dialog box:

Select the chi-square option, leaving a check mark in the associated box. Click "Continue" and then "OK" back in the "Crosstabs" window. This will produce the following SPSS/PASW Statistics output:

satfin SATISFACTION WITH FINANCIAL SITUATION * male Male Dummy Variable Crosstabulation

Count

		male Male Dummy Variable		Total
		0 Female	1 Male	
satfin SATISFACTION WITH FINANCIAL SITUATION	1 SATISFIED	302	271	573
	2 MORE OR LESS	439	380	819
	3 NOT AT ALL SAT	348	276	624
Total		1089	927	2016

Chi-Square Tests

	Value	df	Asymp. Sig. (2-sided)
Pearson Chi-Square	1.225[a]	2	.542
Likelihood Ratio	1.226	2	.542
Linear-by-Linear Association	1.146	1	.284
N of Valid Cases	2016		

a. 0 cells (.0%) have expected count less than 5. The minimum expected count is 263.48.

Note that the chi-square value of 1.225 (2 degrees of freedom) is not statistically significant ($p = 0.542$) according to the results presented in this output.

10

Analysis of Variance

A nalysis of variance (ANOVA) is an inferential statistics technique that involves a statistical test for significance of differences between mean scores of at least two groups across one or more than one variable. ANOVA can be used to test for statistical significance using categorical independent variables in conjunction with a continuous dependent variable. ANOVA is based on the comparison of variance between groups to the variance within groups, emerging as the F ratio, or F statistic.

One-Way ANOVA

We will perform an ANOVA test using "race" as the independent variable and respondent's income as the dependent variable. To measure "race," we will use the recoded, four-category version of that variable. (For details on how to recode "race," see Chapter 2: Transforming Variables.) For income, we will need to recode "rincom06," since it is measured by numeric categories corresponding to nonequivalent ranges of annual earnings. We can use the midpoint dollar amount of each of those ranges to approximate income for respondents in each category. To make it so, follow the following instructions:

TRANSFORM → RECODE INTO DIFFERENT VARIABLES . . .

In the "Recode into Different Variables" dialog box, select "rincom06" and move it from the variable bank on the left over to the area for "Numeric Variable –> Output Variable." Now, type a new name in the Output Variable area, and also a descriptive label. Next, click the "Change" button, and make sure the change was recorded in the Numeric Variable –> Output Variable listing.

At this point, click the "Old and New Values" button, and you will be presented with the following dialog box:

In the "Recode into Different Variables: Old and New Values" dialog box, you will enter the numeric values from the original variable and the corresponding midpoint of each of those ranges as the new values. Don't forget to maintain missing cases properly. The numeric scores on "rincom06" and the appropriate midpoints are displayed in the image above. Notice that for category 25, a true midpoint could not be constructed.

In the example above, the midpoint of each interval is used as an estimate; there are, however, other methods for estimating such intervals. Once you click "Continue" and then "OK" in the prior window, SPSS/PASW Statistics will create your newly coded variable, "rincomMP": respondent's income, range midpoint estimate.

Now, to carry out the one-way ANOVA test, use the following menus:

ANALYZE → COMPARE MEANS → ONE-WAY ANOVA . . .

In the dialog box that is presented, choose the dependent and independent (factor) variables for your analysis. Click the "Options" key to customize your selections further; this will bring up the following dialog box:

Here, descriptive statistics have been requested as well as a plot of the means. Cases have been excluded analysis by analysis. After clicking "Continue" here, and then "OK" in the "One-Way ANOVA" window, SPSS/PASW Statistics will run the test. The output that follows begins with the descriptive statistic information and is followed by the ANOVA results.

Descriptives

rincomMP Resondent's Income, Range Midpoint Estimate

	N	Mean	Std. Deviation	Std. Error	95% Confidence Interval for Mean		Minimum	Maximum
					Lower Bound	Upper Bound		
1 WHITE	824	44279.73	35829.903	1248.194	41829.72	46729.75	500	160000
2 BLACK	162	27916.67	23615.466	1855.406	24252.60	31580.74	500	120000
3 OTHER	51	59186.27	48670.701	6815.261	45497.42	72875.13	500	160000
4 HISPANIC	152	28480.26	25253.820	2048.355	24433.13	32527.40	500	160000
Total	1189	40669.89	34794.254	1009.059	38690.15	42649.63	500	160000

ANOVA

rincomMP Resondent's Income, Range Midpoint Estimate

	Sum of Squares	df	Mean Square	F	Sig.
Between Groups	77156864362.894	3	25718954787.631	22.392	.000
Within Groups	1361083567722.892	1185	1148593728.036		
Total	1438240432085.786	1188			

The F statistic has been calculated at 22.392 with 3 degrees of freedom. Here, F is significant at the $p = 0.000$ level. The means plot has also been provided by SPSS/PASW Statistics as requested and has been reproduced below:

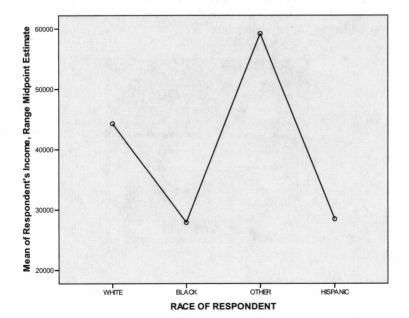

ANOVA in Regression

To examine ANOVA in an ordinary least squares (OLS) regression model, use the following menus:

ANALYZE → REGRESSION → LINEAR . . .

When presented with the "Linear Regression" dialog box, enter your dependent variable and independent variables. To obtain additional partial correlation values or estimates, click the "Statistics" button, and mark the appropriate boxes in that dialog box.

After you click "Continue" in the above dialog box and then "OK" in the "Linear Regression" dialog box, the following output will be presented. Note the sum of squares and mean squares have been provided, as well as the F statistic and its p value (indicating whether it is statistically significant).

Remember that r-square is a PRE (proportional reduction in error) statistic, and when $r^2 = 0.222$, we can interpret that as meaning that 22.2% of the variation in income is explained by variations in education and gender.

Model Summary

Model	R	R Square	Adjusted R Square	Std. Error of the Estimate
1	.471[a]	.222	.220	30722.958

a. Predictors: (Constant), educ HIGHEST YEAR OF SCHOOL COMPLETED, male Male Dummy Variable

Below, you can see that F was calculated at 168.860 with 2 degrees of freedom. This value is statistically significant with $p = 0.000$.

ANOVA[b]

Model		Sum of Squares	df	Mean Square	F	Sig.
1	Regression	318774858322.376	2	159387429161.188	168.860	.000[a]
	Residual	1119465573763.415	1186	943900146.512		
	Total	1438240432085.791	1188			

a. Predictors: (Constant), educ HIGHEST YEAR OF SCHOOL COMPLETED, male Male Dummy Variable

b. Dependent Variable: rincomMP Resondent's Income, Range Midpoint Estimate

As part of the linear regression command, SPSS/PASW Statistics also provides the regression model coefficient output, printed below. Notice that, on average, men are predicted to make almost $18,000/year more than women, and each additional year of education is estimated to bring an average of just under $5,000/year in annual earnings, not controlling for any other factors.

Coefficients[a]

Model		Unstandardized Coefficients		Standardized Coefficients			Correlations		
		B	Std. Error	Beta	t	Sig.	Zero-order	Partial	Part
1	(Constant)	-36910.592	4524.019		-8.159	.000			
	male Male Dummy Variable	17948.875	1785.716	.258	10.051	.000	.234	.280	.257
	educ HIGHEST YEAR OF SCHOOL COMPLETED	4944.312	309.931	.409	15.953	.000	.394	.420	.409

a. Dependent Variable: rincomMP Resondent's Income, Range Midpoint Estimate

11

Editing Output

The SPSS/PASW Statistics Output Editor allows a great degree of freedom for editing charts, tables, and other types of output. This information can all be exported to other computer programs for inclusion in documents created and developed in those programs. Most popular, the information and graphics from SPSS/PASW Statistics can be suitably imported and handled within Microsoft Word, as well as other computer word processing programs.

Editing Basic Tables

The first table below was produced by default by SPSS/PASW Statistics for a "Compare Means" function request for respondents' occupational prestige scores and sex variables, using the following procedure:

ANALYZE → COMPARE MEANS → MEANS . . .

Report

prestg80 RS OCCUPATIONAL PRESTIGE SCORE (1980)

sex RESPONDENTS SEX	Mean	N	Std. Deviation
1 MALE	43.61	895	13.634
2 FEMALE	43.92	1026	14.110
Total	43.77	1921	13.887

The next table has been edited. Labels have been added or edited, and at least one column was resized. You can directly edit the table in the SPSS/PASW Output Viewer window by double-clicking on the table and moving cells, double-clicking and retyping labels, and so on. This is done much the same way that table editing is done using a spreadsheet such as Microsoft Excel. Alternatively, you can use the following menu command:

EDIT → EDIT CONTENT → IN VIEWER . . .

Job Prestige by Gender, GSS 2008

prestg80 RS OCCUPATIONAL PRESTIGE SCORE (1980)

Respondent's Gender	Mean	N	Std. Deviation
1 - MEN	43.61	895	13.634
2 - WOMEN	43.92	1026	14.110
Total	43.77	1921	13.887

If you wish to have the table open in a new window for editing, keeping it separate from all of the other output in your viewer, you can use the following menu options. This can allow more focus on the table being edited.

EDIT → EDIT CONTENT → IN SEPARATE WINDOW . . .

You can also use the SPSS/PASW Statistics pivoting trays function to change the layout of the table if you wish. While the table has been selected for editing, as described above, use the following menus to reveal pivoting trays.

PIVOT → PIVOTING TRAYS

You still have direct access to changing the table in the Output Viewer or separate window, depending on which you have selected. The only difference is that in addition to editing the table itself, you now can avail yourself of the functions in the "Pivoting Trays" window.

The SPSS/PASW Statistics "Pivoting Trays" window gives the user more direct control over the features of the table, including the structure of the variables. This is particularly useful when there are multiple variables in the analysis, including one or more control variables. Interchanging variables using pivoting trays is easy to do and easy to reverse.

Copying to Microsoft Word

There are several options for getting an SPSS/PASW Statistics table into Microsoft Word. One way is to select the table in the SPSS/PASW Output Viewer by clicking on it once. Then copy the table by choosing this menu:

EDIT → COPY

The keyboard shortcut for that function is <Ctrl> + <C> on a Microsoft Windows PC and <APPLE> + <C> on an Apple Macintosh computer.

At this point you can paste the output into your word processor (e.g., Microsoft Word). This can be done by selecting the following menus in Microsoft Word:

EDIT → PASTE

Newer versions of Microsoft Word (Office 2007 for Windows and Office 2008 for Macintosh) have a different menu structure. Simply click the "Paste" icon in the menu bar, or the word "Paste" underneath it. Again, there is a keyboard shortcut for this function: <Ctrl> + <V> on a Windows PC or <APPLE> + <V> on an Apple Computer.

By copying and pasting in this way, you will still be able to edit the tables in Microsoft Word. It can, however, be a bit more cumbersome to do the table editing in Word, and it can also pose layout complications. For instance, resizing the table may necessitate recalibrating font sizes within the table as well as many row and column dimensions. It usually benefits the user to do the table editing in SPSS/PASW Statistics and then, when editing is complete, to copy the table into a document, where it can be resized proportionally, like a photo or other object. To do this, select the following menus in Microsoft Word (or similar menus in another word processing program):

EDIT → PASTE SPECIAL...

Then double click "Picture" in the "Paste Special" box that appears. This will paste the table into the document as a largely noneditable (but resizable) object. While the internal characteristics of the table can no longer be changed at this point, placement and sizing of the table is much more convenient this way.

Newer versions of Microsoft Word (Office 2007 for Windows and Office 2008 for Macintosh) have a different menu structure. With the "Home" menu tab selected, click the arrow under "Paste" in the upper left corner of the screen and choose "Paste Special" from the pull down menu that appears.

Exporting Output

It is possible to have SPSS/PASW Statistics automatically export the elements of an output file into separate objects that can be used individually or read into some other program (e.g., a word processor). Another option is to transform the output file in its entirety into another document type for use with another editing/graphics program or word processing program. To do this, follow the following menus:

FILE → EXPORT . . .

Under "Objects to Export," select what to export: all output, all visible output, or selected output. If you want to export only selected items, you must click on them to highlight them in the Output Viewer prior to opening the "Export Output" window. In the example above, "Selected" is dimmed, and therefore not an option, since no output was selected in the Output Viewer before the "Export Output" dialog box was opened.

In the Document area, select the format in which you would like the exported files to be saved. Also, in the "File Name" area, you have the option to name the directory where the new files will be saved, if the default location is not satisfactory.

If, in the Document area, you select "Graphics only," the lower part of the window under "Graphics" will no longer be dimmed, and you can select the type of graphic file to which SPSS/PASW Statistics will write your output. You can choose from the list of file types. For example, if you select "JPEG," all of the charts and tables will be saved as separate *.JPG files, which can be then be opened with or imported into other programs and handled like graphic objects.

Editing Charts and Graphs

The SPSS/PASW Statistics Output Viewer allows for interactive editing of charts and graphs. Not only can labels, titles, numbers, legends, and so forth be added and edited, but the very type and style of the chart or graph can be changed from the output interface.

Suppose you create a clustered bar graph, like the one that is created below:

GRAPHS → CHART BUILDER . . .

For this graph, we wish to examine the dependent variable, "cappun" (opinion about capital punishment/favoring or opposing the death penalty for murder) as distributed across race/ethnicity and gender. We will use race and sex, respectively, to analyze those dimensions. This version of "race" is the recoded version, including information from the variable

"Hispanic." For details on how this variable was recoded, see Chapter 2: Transforming Variables. The race recode is specifically dealt with in the following section of the chapter: "Recoding Using Two or More Variables to Create a New Variable."

Click "OK" to produce the bar graph. Now, for a more comprehensive and interactive way to edit the bar graph (or any other SPSS/PASW Statistics chart or graph), select and double click the chart or graph. A new "Chart Editor" window will pop up, as pictured below:

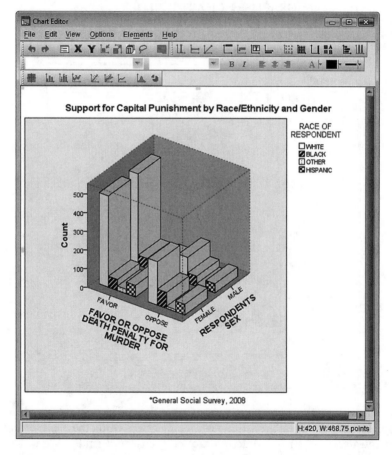

Note that the chart is shown above using patterns to differentiate columns, rather than color. Patterns are particularly useful for printing monochrome output, such as that produced on a black and white laser printer. Color charts are the default, unless you change the preferences settings for SPSS/PASW Statistics using the "Options" box, as seen below:

EDIT → OPTIONS . . .

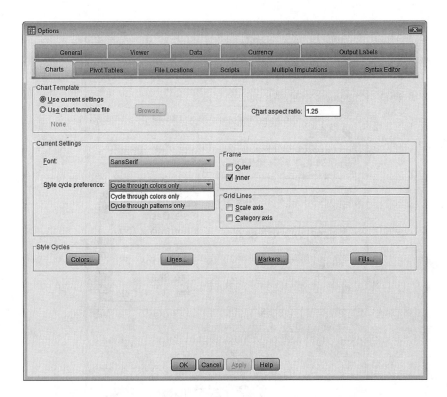

However, even if you have not changed the default from color to patterns, there is no need to scrap your work. You can switch from color to patterns (or the other way around) by using the Properties window. See the illustration of the Properties window after the next paragraph for details on exactly how to perform the switch.

Numerous editing options are available in the Properties window, which usually opens automatically with the "Chart Editor" but can also be accessed by selecting the following menus:

EDIT → PROPERTIES

You can also reach the "Properties" box by using the shortcuts <Ctrl> + <T> on a Windows PC or <APPLE> + <T> on a Macintosh.

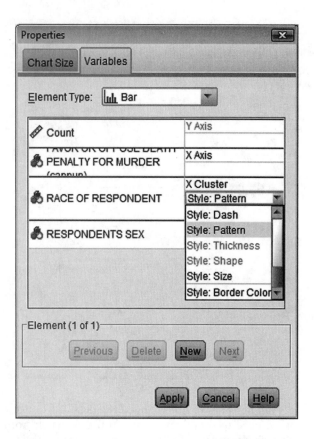

Using the pull down menu for "Element Type," you can change the type of graph in the output, from a bar graph, for example, to some other type of graph, like a pie chart or an area graph. It is not necessary to go through and rerun the graph/chart function. It can be rebuilt directly from the "Chart Editor."

By selecting "Style" by the X Cluster variable, "race of respondent," you can choose whether to have the graph in color, black and white patterns, or some other method of illustration. For this example, the "pattern" style was chosen over the color option, as is often best for a monochrome printer output.

A title has been added by selecting OPTIONS → TITLE . . . from the "Chart Editor" window. Here, a text box will be added to the top area of the "Chart Editor" with the word "title"; simply replace that word with what you would like to title your chart. A footnote to indicate the source of data used to create the graph has been added by selecting: OPTIONS → FOOT- NOTE . . . Here, a text box will be added to the bottom area of the "Chart Editor" with the word "footnote"; replace this with the appropriate foot- note. Here, the data come from the 2008 General Social Survey.

Also, notice that the graph has been rotated vertically, so that we can better see the bars in the back row. You can change the vertical and horizontal rotations on the overall image by using the following menus:

EDIT → 3-D ROTATION

For this example, the vertical rotation was augmented to 30 degrees, but you can change it to whatever works best with your image.

12

Advanced Applications

Merging Data From Multiple Files

There are typically two ways a user wants to merge files. One way is to combine two data files that contain the same variables, but consist of different cases (e.g., two or more waves of surveys completed by different people, but including the same information). Another way is to have additional variables to add to existing cases (e.g., second round of responses from the same respondents). Note that you must be doing this from the Data Editor window containing the file (active dataset) to which you wish to add cases or variables.

First, suppose you want to add cases:

DATA → MERGE FILES → ADD CASES ...

If you have already opened the data file in another SPSS/PASW Statistics Data Editor window, then you can select "An open dataset" and choose from the list that will appear. Otherwise, select "An external

SPSS/PASW Statistics data file," and locate the file you wish to add. Both files, of course, need to be in SPSS/PASW (*.sav) format. If the file you are adding is not in SPSS/PASW data format, then you should first import that file into SPSS/PASW Statistics before carrying out the merge function. For more information about importing files, see Chapter 1 of this book.

You will be presented with a new dialog box, like the one that follows:

Assuming there are no unpaired variables, or you are not concerned with pairing variables (same variables in two different datasets each with a different name), select "OK," and SPSS/PASW Statistics will perform the addition of cases to your data file.

Now, suppose you want to add new variables to your dataset:

FILE → DATA → ADD VARIABLES . . .

Again, select the appropriate file, whether it is open in another instance (window) of SPSS/PASW Statistics, or it is located on a disk or server connected to your computer. Click "Continue," and you will be presented with the next dialog box:

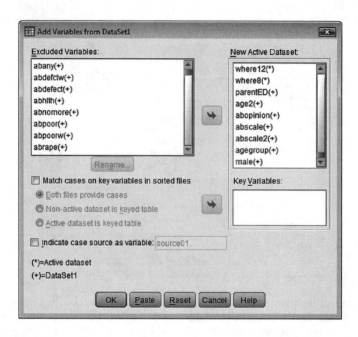

The "New Active Dataset" box shows the variables that will be contained in the newly merged data file. The excluded variables are those that are duplicates in name. If any of those are not duplicates, but happen to have the same name, then select each one and click the "Rename" button to correct the problem. If you are not certain that the cases are listed in the same order in the two data files, then you must match the cases by some identifying variable (e.g., a case ID): Select the variable that contains that information, and move it into the "Key Variables" box. Click "OK," and SPSS/PASW Statistics will perform the merge as instructed.

Opening Previously Created Syntax Files

Syntax files provide computer code to instruct SPSS/PASW Statistics to perform functions. Most of these functions can be achieved by using the point-and-click method that this book uses. That is, functions can be performed by using the menus at the top of the Data Editor window. Creating syntax code using SPSS/PASW Statistics syntax computer language is not addressed in this book. If you have an SPSS/PASW Statistics syntax file, however, with code for performing SPSS/PASW commands, open it as follows:

FILE → OPEN → SYNTAX

You will get a dialog box like the one below:

Navigate your computer files, locate your file, and open it. The syntax code will appear in a "Syntax Editor" window, like the one that follows. Select the portion of the code that you wish to run. (The example below runs frequency information on a data file that is supposed to already be opened.) Click the "run" button to execute the computer code. (The "run" button is the blue triangle.) You can also type <Ctrl> + r (<Apple> + r for Macintosh computers) or select from the menu:

RUN → SELECTION

From the menu, you also have the option to run the whole file or to run it from a particular point to the end. The menus also afford the option to choose which lines (from, to) of syntax code to run.

Creating New SPSS/PASW Syntax Files

While this book will not provide detailed information about creating syntax files, there are a few things about syntax files that may be useful, even for those users who have no intention of writing code to perform SPSS/PASW Statistics functions. To create a new syntax file, select the following menu options:

FILE → NEW → SYNTAX

A new window, Syntax Editor, will appear. Information that is typed into this interface will form the syntax file. All or part of what is typed into this interface can be used either immediately or at a later time.

With any of the SPSS/PASW Statistics point-and-click functions—those operations implemented using the menus at the top of the editor windows—there is an option to select "Paste" instead of clicking "OK." When you do this, SPSS/PASW Statistics does not execute the function; instead, it records the instructions for performing the function in a syntax window. A user may choose to save the instructions for later use, or run them immediately and save a copy for future use or reference. What is pasted are the instructions that SPSS/PASW Statistics gives "behind the scenes" for that particular function (e.g., frequency distributions). Saving the commands in this way allows faster replication of a series of tasks.

Saving pasted SPSS/PASW Statistics syntax files can be useful for those who are performing many operations that are repetitive or similar across variables—particularly if they are more complicated functions. Take recoding variables, for instance. If you are recoding a number of variables with similar, but not identical, schemes, then by pasting and editing one recode command, you could potentially save a lot of time.

Saving syntax files also provides a complete record of how a data file was altered, which can be helpful to some users, since SPSS/PASW Statistics will show the altered data file only and not provide a list of updates that have been made.

About the Author

William E. Wagner, III, PhD, is an Associate Professor of sociology at California State University, Channel Islands. Prior to coming to CSU, Channel Islands, he served as a member of the faculty and director of the Institute for Social and Community Research at California State University, Bakersfield. He completed his PhD in sociology at the University of Illinois, Chicago. Dr. Wagner also holds an undergraduate degree in mathematics from St. Mary's College of Maryland. He has published in national and regional scholarly journals on topics such as urban sociology, sports, homophobia, and academic status. Dr. Wagner is coauthor of the seventh edition of *Adventures in Social Research*, published by Pine Forge Press (2010).

Supporting researchers for more than 40 years

Research methods have always been at the core of SAGE's publishing program. Founder Sara Miller McCune published SAGE's first methods book, *Public Policy Evaluation*, in 1970. Soon after, she launched the *Quantitative Applications in the Social Sciences* series—affectionately known as the "little green books."

Always at the forefront of developing and supporting new approaches in methods, SAGE published early groundbreaking texts and journals in the fields of qualitative methods and evaluation.

Today, more than 40 years and two million little green books later, SAGE continues to push the boundaries with a growing list of more than 1,200 research methods books, journals, and reference works across the social, behavioral, and health sciences. Its imprints—Pine Forge Press, home of innovative textbooks in sociology, and Corwin, publisher of PreK–12 resources for teachers and administrators—broaden SAGE's range of offerings in methods. SAGE further extended its impact in 2008 when it acquired CQ Press and its best-selling and highly respected political science research methods list.

From qualitative, quantitative, and mixed methods to evaluation, SAGE is the essential resource for academics and practitioners looking for the latest methods by leading scholars.

For more information, visit **www.sagepub.com**.